W9-CDJ-798

WHISKY
IT'S NOT ROCKET SCIENCE

Mickaël Guidot

Illustrations by Yannis Varoutsikos

WHISKY
IT'S NOT ROCKET SCIENCE

hamlyn

ACKNOWLEDGEMENTS

From the author
Thanks to my darling Dima, who intoxicates me
every single day; to my parents, for their support
through all my various projects (and for looking
after all my bottles); Yannis, for his jokes; Charlotte
and the Marabout team, who have supported
me uncomplainingly; and all those who have
contributed to my blog, ForGeorges. Thanks
to all the experts who have been interviewed
for this book for agreeing to share part of their
knowledge and passion: Nicolas Julhès, Jonas
Vallat, Guillaume Charnier, Ophelia Deroy, Jim
Beveridge, Christophe Gremeaux, Émilie Pineau,
Guillaume Charnier...and all those I have left out.

From the illustrator
To my grandfather, Bubu, who actually
introduced me to pastis rather than whisky.
But, as you have to try everything a first
time, it was not bad at all! Thanks to you,
Mickaël, for all these great discoveries and
these first steps in the world of whisky.

CONTENTS

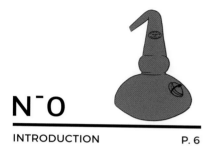

Dedicated to my grandfather, Georges, who introduced me to whisky for the first time, and who remains our guide throughout this book.

N⁻O
INTRODUCTION

W hisky: a drink reserved for elites, where just a handful of international experts can go on and on about it using all the usual pompous phrases? That may be the myth, but these days the reality is very different. We all have some kind of opinion on whisky, positive or negative, whether we are occasional drinkers or simply know people who are. But to get any further into it requires help: just a bit of advice or explanation that can enable us to figure out what kind of drinks we actually like.

As a young man, I was lucky enough to get a chance to discover this world during family gatherings at the home of my grandfather, Georges. He took the time to get me to taste and understand what I was drinking, and I began to realize that the best drinks of all owed their quality to two things: the best-quality ingredients, grown on the land; and the skills and craftsmanship of the people who created them.

Many years later, I created the blog ForGeorges. The idea was to avoid the usual pompous kind of discussions that tend to crop up on tasting blogs, and instead to try to engage as many people as possible with the fascinating world of whisky.

So don't expect an expert work full of tasting notes and complicated words here. However, if you would simply like help in choosing your next whisky or whiskies, or to understand the sensations that hit you when you taste, or to discover the fascinating world of whisky production, then you have come to the right place. My grandfather, Georges, though the passion he handed down to me, will be your guide.

WHISKY: WHO DRINKS IT?

If you thought whisky drinkers were all retired businessmen who play golf, own an Aston Martin and wear a kilt, then think again!

Forget the clichés portrayed in films and novels. Whisky drinkers, in this first quarter of the 21st century, are an eclectic bunch. Many people – perhaps yourself included – have had a bad whisky experience. But don't give up. As Grandfather Georges liked to say, 'You can't not like whisky. You just haven't found the whisky that suits you yet.'

With so many whiskies on this planet, it is just a matter of discovering the one that is right for you: a drink you start to like, then love – and become attached to for the rest of your life. And if you think you are already there, then keep on looking anyway. You may discover yet another that you grow to love even more.

THE URBAN MILLENNIAL

While gin, vodka and rum have long been the spirits of choice in most urban bars, whisky is making a comeback. In trendy districts across the world, from Tokyo to Brooklyn via Paris, it is impossible not to find a whisky bar packed with millennials enjoying a carefully curated range of spirits, often sourced from micro-distilleries in countries less well-known for their whisky.

THE FEMALE DRINKER

Whisky is a man's drink, right? Wrong. In fact, women make up around 30 per cent of all whisky drinkers worldwide. Often discovering the taste for the first time in a cocktail bar, women tend to be pigeonholed by whisky marketing departments (see below) as favouring the more mellow, fruity whiskies, though like all whisky drinkers, most will go on to try out more challenging and complex tastes.

Here are just a few of the personality types who have joined the ranks of whisky drinkers in recent years.

 SO ARE THERE SPECIFIC WHISKIES FOR WOMEN?

Knowing that women like to drink whisky has led some brands to target female consumers specifically, usually with whiskies that they can describe as 'light' or 'fruity', on the assumption that this is the kind of whisky women want. Of course, these whisky characteristics appeal to male drinkers too.

THE WINE BUFF

People who know about wine can easily appreciate what it takes to create great whisky. As with viniculture, making whisky needs time and care throughout the process, with the role of a cellar-master at a whisky distillery being rather like that of a sommelier. You could even say that a single malt is akin to a Bourgogne Pinot Noir, while a blended whisky would be more like a blended Bordeaux. Another similarity is in the importance of high-quality casks. It is not unusual to find distilleries using casks from prestigious French wineries during the finishing process of some of their whiskies.

THE FOODIE

Whisky has traditionally been seen either as an apéritif or as a digestif: something to be enjoyed either before or after a meal. These days, it is also showing up during the meal itself, either as an accompanying beverage (replacing wine) or used in the kitchen as part of a recipe. At its best, whisky can give a familiar dish an exciting new twist. Not surprisingly, the most edgy and adventurous chefs are leading the way.

THE COCKTAIL FAN

The most conservative whisky buffs may tut in disapproval, but cocktails based on whisky are making a bit of a comeback. The whisky-quaffing creative director Don Draper, in the TV series, *Mad Men* was a fan of the Old-Fashioned and may have helped get the trend going again. And please, repeat after me: a whisky-and-coke is not a cocktail!

TYPES OF WHISKY

Whiskies have different names depending on two main factors: where they come from, and the type of grain used to make them. This may sound like we're getting into some rather geeky territory, but stay with us. There are just three main types of whisky (opposite) and only two possible ways to spell it.

WHISKY

Scotland,
Japan, France

OR

Ireland,
United States of America

WHISKEY

WHISKY OR WHISKEY?

If you are reading this book in Ireland or the USA, then you will be used to seeing the word 'whiskey' spelled with an 'e'. Anywhere else in the world, it's whisky. Is it just a common mistake? Not at all. When the spirit in question is made in Scotland, Japan, France or elsewhere, it is called – and usually spelled – 'whisky'. If it is made in the USA or Ireland, the spelling 'whiskey' is generally correct. The reasons are historical. In the 19th century, the quality of Scottish whisky was extremely variable – and often downright awful. Many

Irish producers, aiming to differentiate their single-malt products from cheaper grain and single-malt Scottish blends, decided to add an 'e' and call it 'whiskey' prior to shipping to the United States. Since then, the name 'whiskey' gradually became the standard for whiskies produced in Ireland and the USA – although there remain several exceptions. In this book, we will use the spelling whisky (or whiskies) when talking about whisky in general terms, and whiskey (and whiskeys) when referring to Irish or American spirits.

+ **=**

SINGLE MALT

Single malt is produced in just one whisky distillery and, historically, it is regarded as the original whisky of the Scottish Highlands. It is made exclusively with malted barley, which is distilled in pot stills. In cases where a producer mixes several single malts from different distilleries (without involving grain whiskies), the result is a blended malt whisky.

GRAIN WHISKY

It is rare to find a bottle of grain whisky on the market, as it is used mainly to make blended whiskies. That said, a few brands still have 'grain whisky' on their labels, usually the result of a continuous distillation process using corn, wheat and barley (which may or may not be malted). While grain whisky is generally considered less complex in flavour than most single malts, some excellent bottles of the former can be found if you look hard enough.

BLENDED WHISKY

Blended whisky is the best-known and most commonly found whisky in the world, and accounts for 90 per cent of Scotch whisky production. Some of the biggest international brands, such as Johnny Walker, Chivas or Ballantine's, are blended whiskies, and the blending process can created whiskies that are harmonious in taste while being lighter and generally less costly than most single malts. There are, of course, exceptions to every rule in whisky, and there are also many luxury blends of exceptional quality.

 IS ONE TYPE OF WHISKY BETTER THAN ANOTHER?

Considered by many aficionados as the Rolls Royce of whisky, single malt is often thought to be better than the rest, and the price premium it commands supports this belief. However, some whisky experts, not to mention blind tastings, disagree that single malts have the edge. There is no 'better' whisky, only different ones. End of.

WHO INVENTED WHISKY?

It's Ireland versus Scotland – not, however, in a Six Nations rugby championship,
but in a battle over which of these two nations can claim to have invented whisky.
Let's take a look at the origins, myths and reality.

IRELAND *VS* SCOTLAND

NAME:
Ireland

SURFACE AREA:
84,421 km^2

POPULATION:
6.3 million

CLIMATE:
Oceanic

RUGBY EMBLEM:
The clover

SIX–NATIONS
GRAND SLAMS WON: 3

ANTHEM:
Ireland's Call
and *Amhrán na bhFiann*
(home games)

NAME:
Scotland

SURFACE AREA:
78,772 km^2

POPULATION:
5.3 million

CLIMATE:
Temperate

RUGBY EMBLEM:
The thistle

SIX–NATIONS
GRAND SLAMS WON: 3

ANTHEM:
Flower of Scotland

WITH THE TWO SIDES LOOKING EVENLY BALANCED, DOES ONE HAVE HISTORY ON ITS SIDE?
IT IS GOING TO BE A CLOSE-FOUGHT MATCH.

UISGE BEATHA: THE WATER OF LIFE

Both the Scottish Gaelic *uisge beatha* and Irish *uisce beatha* literally mean *eau de vie* or 'water of life', a term first coined, somewhat optimistically, by monks. They had observed during experiments that the bodies of their deceased brethren remained preserved for long periods in eau de vie – at that time a distilled liquid made with honey and herbs that became widely used as a medicine, although it would have tasted quite unlike anything we know today as whisky. Its reputation was somewhat tarnished near the beginning of the 15th century, when an Irish clan chief drank too much water of life and died – 'water of death' might have been more apt.

The legend of Saint Patrick

While there is no written evidence to prove it, the Irish are convinced that the existence of whisky is all down to an evangelist otherwise known as Saint Patrick, whose annual saint's day celebrations on 17 March often involve alcohol. During the 5th century, when Europe was being invaded by the Barbarian hordes, Ireland became a place of refuge for Christian monks, who brought with them a good deal of what we could now call scientific knowledge, some of which led to the invention of distillation. From this came *uisce beatha* – the Celtic term for distilled alcohol, or 'water of life.' The Scots don't dispute this version of events – although they do point out that Saint Patrick was Scottish!

0 - 0
Ball is centred

When England comes into play

A third player crashed the party during the 12th century, when England invaded Ireland. Henry II and his soldiers discovered a local liquor that was getting everyone extremely drunk: the famous *uisce beatha*. The only problem with this story is that there is no written record of it either.

1 - 0
to Ireland

The clash of Islay

In 1300, the Mac Beatha family – a rich and cultured bunch who were passionate about the study of science and medicine – settled on the small Scottish island of Islay. When the Scottish King James IV went to war against the Lord of Islay, he discovered their stocks of alcohol: *uisce beatha*, aka the 'water of life' – or, more simply, the water of the Beatha clan, making the Beathas the people who invented whisky. This legend persists to this day, giving the Island of Islay a claim to being the birthplace of whisky.

1 - 1
Scotland equalizes

Written evidence emerges

One of the first written records of a beverage resembling whisky in the British Isles appeared in 14th-century Ireland, when Bishop Richard Ledred wrote a manuscript known as the *Red Book of Ossory*. In addition to religious hymns and administrative texts, the book includes a recipe for a distilled spirit known as *aqua vitae* – Latin for 'water of life' – but this one was based on wine.

2 - 1
to Ireland

Scotland refuses to be sidelined

According to the Scottish national archives, mention is made in 1494 of a distilled spirit based on malted barley – proof, if it were needed, of the existence of malt whisky in Scotland at the time. The archives refer to a Benedictine monk receiving a supply of malt to make *aqua vitae* by order of the king.

2 - 2
Draw

England returns to the game

Not until 1736 did an English captain use the word 'usky', which later becomes modern 'whisky' in correspondences, and links it with the Scots. 'The pride of Scotland', he wrote, 'is usky.'

The final score?

It's impossible to say. Even Grandfather Georges didn't have the answer, and truthfully, nobody does. Basically, it's like supporting a sports team: you simply choose a side and buy into the myth. Alternatively, hedge your bets. If you're with Scots, tell them you think Scotland invented whisky. And if you're drinking in Ireland, say it was the Irish. At least you will make more friends during your tastings.

WHISKY GOES GLOBAL

Whenever you talk about whisky, you can't help thinking about Scotland. Just think how common it is for someone to walk into a bar and ask for 'Scotch' when ordering a whisky. But the global whisky scene is changing fast. Fasten your seatbelts for a quick world tour.

THE USA AND CANADA

A vast expanse of wilderness, mountains and prairies; cities and skyscrapers; cowboys...and plenty of whisky distilleries! Whether it's making bourbon or rye on a global scale or in micro-distilleries, the North American whiskey market has a strong history and is more vibrant than ever.

IRELAND

Ireland: a beautiful land of rocky coastlines, cinematic landscapes and pints of Guinness. What is often overlooked is how much Ireland dominated the global whiskey market in the 19th century, in particular via exports to the United States. Are its glory days over? Or are they making a comeback? The verdict is still undecided.

SCOTLAND

In addition to kilts and sheep, this country has the greatest number of single-malt distilleries in the world: more than a hundred of them. This abundance of production is divided into five distinct regions: Speyside, the Highlands, the Lowlands, Islay and Campbeltown, and the Islands.

There are no geographical restrictions for where you can produce whisky, as long as it meets the specific 'spiritual' requirements: in other words, it must be made from distilled alcohol based on malted (or non-malted) grains. If you want to set up a distillery in your garden tomorrow, you will be able to start making whisky. There is even an excellent whisky that comes from Tasmania!

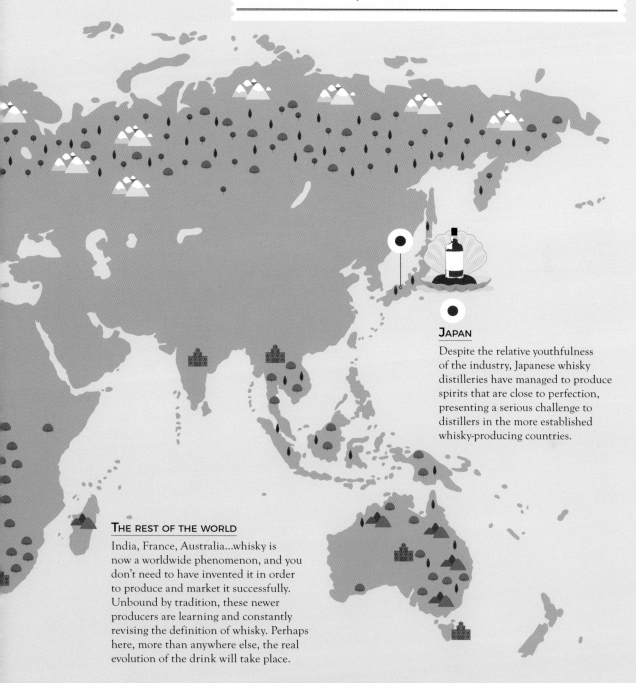

JAPAN

Despite the relative youthfulness of the industry, Japanese whisky distilleries have managed to produce spirits that are close to perfection, presenting a serious challenge to distillers in the more established whisky-producing countries.

THE REST OF THE WORLD

India, France, Australia...whisky is now a worldwide phenomenon, and you don't need to have invented it in order to produce and market it successfully. Unbound by tradition, these newer producers are learning and constantly revising the definition of whisky. Perhaps here, more than anywhere else, the real evolution of the drink will take place.

THE WHISKY TIMELINE

The history of whisky is a complex one, with the story unfolding, sometimes simultaneously, in various parts of the world, often in completely unrelated ways. Here are some key dates and events.

◀ 5th to 14th centuries
Invention of distillation and the production of *uisce beatha*

1608
The Bushmills region is authorized to distil whisky

1500

1600

1700

1750

1494
First written reference to *aqua vitae* in Scotland

1505
Barber-surgeons are the only people licensed in Edinburgh to distil *aqua vitae*

1644
First taxes on alcohol in Scotland

1724
A 'malt tax' is imposed, and major strikes break out in Edinburgh and Glasgow

1759
Birth of Robert Burns, renowned Scottish poet and whisky drinker

1784
The Wash Act comes into effect creating a border between the Lowlands and the Highlands; taxes in the Highlands are calculated according to still size and are lower

1781
Distillation on unlicensed stills is banned

1783
Evan Williams (a pioneer of bourbon) founds his distillery in Kentucky

1791
Excise Whiskey Tax voted into law, leading to emergence of illegal moonshine and the 'Whiskey Rebellion'

1794
George Washington sends 12,500 men to Pennsylvania to quell the Whiskey Rebellion

1671
The first still arrives in Quebec City, Canada

1736
First appearance of the word 'whisky'

1755
The word 'whisky' enters the famous dictionary compiled by Dr Samuel Johnson in London

1872
First evidence of Scotch whisky in Japan ▼

1853
The fleet of American Commodore Mathew Perry disembarks in the bay of Tokyo with casks of bourbon in the hold

1923
Yamazaki builds the first whisky distillery in Japan ▼

1918
Masataka Taketsuru arrives in Scotland to learn about the whisky-making process

IRELAND

1980
The Irish Whiskey Act becomes law ▼

1831
Aeneas Coffey fine-tunes Robert Stein's still and applies for a patent ▼

1826
Irishman Robert Stein applies for a patent for his continuous column still. The Irish are sceptical and, ultimately, the Scots commercialize it successfully ▼

1966
Creation of Irish Distillers, which merges the remaining distilleries in Ireland ▼

▲1800 ▲1850 ▲1900 ▲1950 ▲2000

SCOTLAND

▲ **1823**
With the Excise Act, the United Kingdom tries to stop whisky smuggling by charging small-scale distillers a licence fee to declare their activities and pay excise duties

▲ **1820**
Launch of the Johnny Walker brand

▲ **1843**
Chivas becomes the official supplier of Queen Victoria

▲ **1909**
Thanks to a royal commission, both single malts and blends can now be known as 'whisky'

▲ **1933**
The first legal definition of Scotch whisky is published

▲ **1960**
Creation of the Scotch Whisky Association

▲ **1915**
Whisky has to be aged in a warehouse for two years, increased to three years in 1916

USA

▲ **1820**
Invention of charcoal filtration to purify whiskey

▲ **1798**
The state of Kentucky has more than 200 distilleries

▲ **1920**
Start of national prohibition in the USA

▲ **1964**
The US Congress recognizes bourbon whiskey as a 'distinctive product of the United States'

THE WORLD

▲ **1841**
Old wine bottles are used to distribute whisky to grocers

▲ **1887**
Publication of the first book on the distilleries of the United Kingdom, by Alfred Barnard

▲ **1863**
Arrival of the phylloxera outbreak, which destroys many of the vineyards in France

The whisky timeline

THE MYSTERIES
OF THE WHISKY STILL

Strange and fascinating, and above all an object of great beauty, the copper still is an iconic part of the whisky-making tradition.

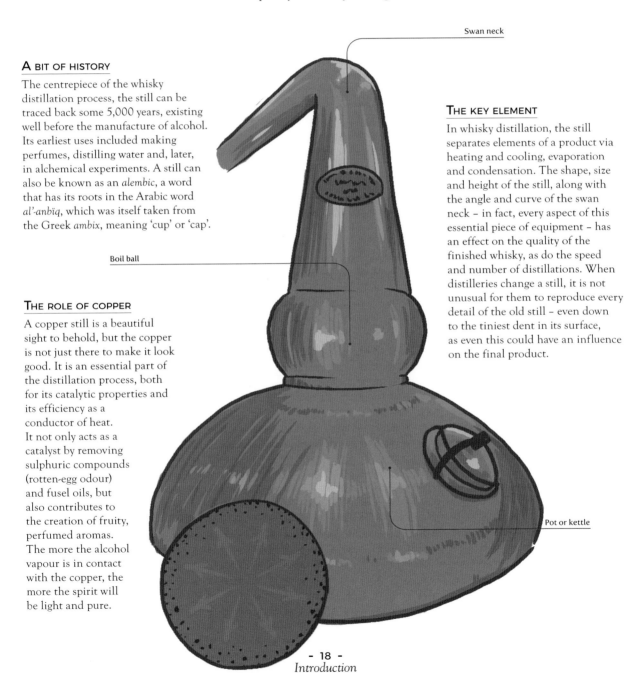

Swan neck

Boil ball

Pot or kettle

A BIT OF HISTORY

The centrepiece of the whisky distillation process, the still can be traced back some 5,000 years, existing well before the manufacture of alcohol. Its earliest uses included making perfumes, distilling water and, later, in alchemical experiments. A still can also be known as an *alembic*, a word that has its roots in the Arabic word *al'-anbīq*, which was itself taken from the Greek *ambix*, meaning 'cup' or 'cap'.

THE ROLE OF COPPER

A copper still is a beautiful sight to behold, but the copper is not just there to make it look good. It is an essential part of the distillation process, both for its catalytic properties and its efficiency as a conductor of heat. It not only acts as a catalyst by removing sulphuric compounds (rotten-egg odour) and fusel oils, but also contributes to the creation of fruity, perfumed aromas. The more the alcohol vapour is in contact with the copper, the more the spirit will be light and pure.

THE KEY ELEMENT

In whisky distillation, the still separates elements of a product via heating and cooling, evaporation and condensation. The shape, size and height of the still, along with the angle and curve of the swan neck – in fact, every aspect of this essential piece of equipment – has an effect on the quality of the finished whisky, as do the speed and number of distillations. When distilleries change a still, it is not unusual for them to reproduce every detail of the old still – even down to the tiniest dent in its surface, as even this could have an influence on the final product.

DIFFERENT STILL TYPES

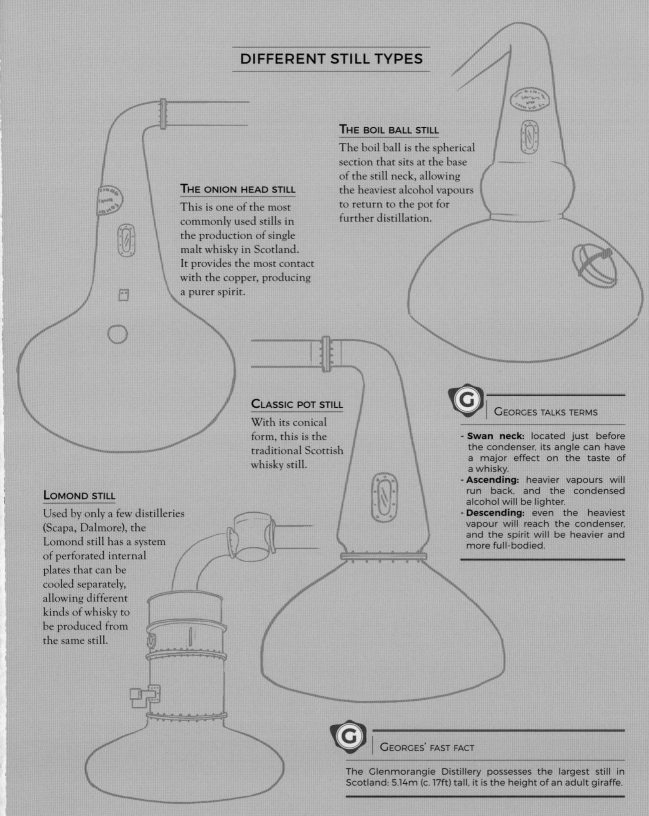

THE ONION HEAD STILL

This is one of the most commonly used stills in the production of single malt whisky in Scotland. It provides the most contact with the copper, producing a purer spirit.

THE BOIL BALL STILL

The boil ball is the spherical section that sits at the base of the still neck, allowing the heaviest alcohol vapours to return to the pot for further distillation.

CLASSIC POT STILL

With its conical form, this is the traditional Scottish whisky still.

LOMOND STILL

Used by only a few distilleries (Scapa, Dalmore), the Lomond still has a system of perforated internal plates that can be cooled separately, allowing different kinds of whisky to be produced from the same still.

GEORGES TALKS TERMS

- **Swan neck:** located just before the condenser, its angle can have a major effect on the taste of a whisky.
- **Ascending:** heavier vapours will run back, and the condensed alcohol will be lighter.
- **Descending:** even the heaviest vapour will reach the condenser, and the spirit will be heavier and more full-bodied.

GEORGES' FAST FACT

The Glenmorangie Distillery possesses the largest still in Scotland: 5.14m (c. 17ft) tall, it is the height of an adult giraffe.

The mysteries of the whisky still

N°1
AT THE DISTILLERY

Is whisky in the 21st century the product of a highly automated process, perfected over time with advances in manufacturing technology? Not entirely. Many distillers still rely on their senses of sight, taste, smell and touch to produce quality whisky. Put on your walking shoes, Georges is about to take you on a tour of the distillery!

THE INGREDIENTS

Some distilleries swear that their choice of water is what brings a unique taste to their whisky, others that it is down to the quality of their barley. One thing is certain: it is impossible to work out how much each ingredient influences the final taste. As with any great recipe, it is the alchemy of the ingredients that makes for a great result.

THE GRAINS

Buying grains for the malting process is one of the most expensive steps in whisky production. For single malt, the choice of barley is crucial. While some distilleries employ staff who are involved in selecting and malting barley on site, others rely on third-party malting companies, often large-scale operations where barley is processed into malt under carefully controlled conditions to ensure that the quality is the same every year. In most cases, the barley in Scotch whisky is imported from suppliers across the border in England, or from South Africa and other countries.

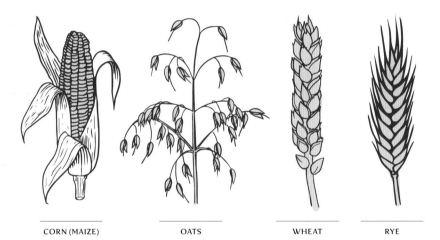

| BARLEY | CORN (MAIZE) | OATS | WHEAT | RYE |

However, barley does not have the monopoly. Other whiskies are made using corn (or maize), such as bourbon. Rye is used to make – you guessed it – rye whiskey, and other whiskies can be made with wheat, oats or even other, rarer grains such as spelt. Barley, however, provides the largest range of aromas.

BAD BARLEY = BAD WHISKY

Selecting barley is a crucial part of the expertise required to make whisky. If barley is too rich in proteins, it should not be sold to a distillery. If it contains traces of mildew, it won't be usable as the mould could taint the resulting whisky.

02

Water

'Water is whisky's best friend,' so the saying goes. Many Scots are convinced that the quality and purity of their water are essential for making a great whisky. But this belief is difficult to justify, given that water only contributes approximately less than five per cent to the eventual taste of whisky. What is clear, however, is that it plays a key role in malting and distillation, and also at the bottling stage. The quantities of water used in whisky production are, frankly, astonishing.

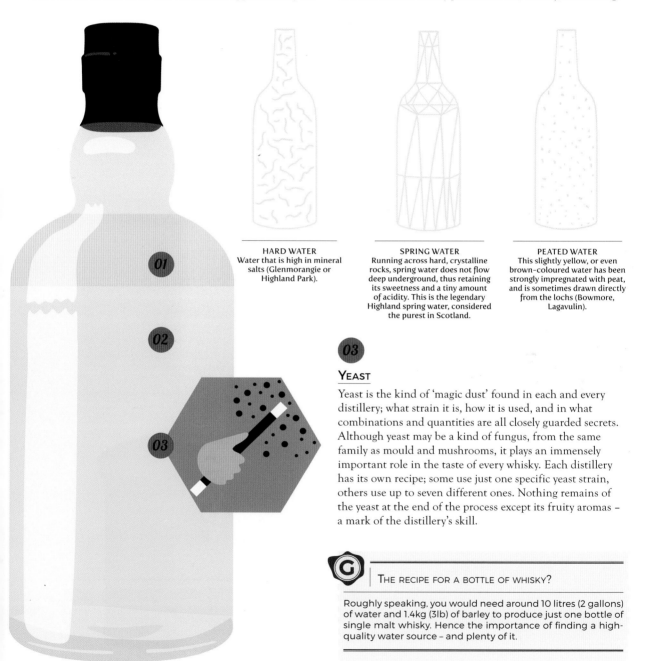

HARD WATER
Water that is high in mineral salts (Glenmorangie or Highland Park).

SPRING WATER
Running across hard, crystalline rocks, spring water does not flow deep underground, thus retaining its sweetness and a tiny amount of acidity. This is the legendary Highland spring water, considered the purest in Scotland.

PEATED WATER
This slightly yellow, or even brown-coloured water has been strongly impregnated with peat, and is sometimes drawn directly from the lochs (Bowmore, Lagavulin).

03

Yeast

Yeast is the kind of 'magic dust' found in each and every distillery; what strain it is, how it is used, and in what combinations and quantities are all closely guarded secrets. Although yeast may be a kind of fungus, from the same family as mould and mushrooms, it plays an immensely important role in the taste of every whisky. Each distillery has its own recipe; some use just one specific yeast strain, others use up to seven different ones. Nothing remains of the yeast at the end of the process except its fruity aromas – a mark of the distillery's skill.

G | THE RECIPE FOR A BOTTLE OF WHISKY?

Roughly speaking, you would need around 10 litres (2 gallons) of water and 1.4kg (3lb) of barley to produce just one bottle of single malt whisky. Hence the importance of finding a high-quality water source – and plenty of it.

THE SEVEN STAGES OF PRODUCTION

It only takes three ingredients to make whisky: barley (or another grain), yeast and water. However, the production process is complex, with seven distinct stages. Mastering each of these determines the final quality of the whisky.

01
MALTING

Once the barley has been harvested, malting it becomes the first essential step in whisky-making. Most distilleries leave this to specialist industrial malting facilities rather than doing it in-house. The aim is to extract starch from the barley via four stages, beginning with soaking then, finally, drying it. For peated malt, the barley is dried over the smoke of a peat fire.

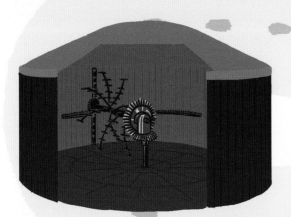

02
BREWING

The malt is crushed to create a coarse flour – the grist – that is mixed with hot water in a large tank called the mash tun to create a thick paste. Stirring the mixture continuously helps the water extract the sugars, which are used in the following stage.

03
FERMENTATION

The water containing the sugars (the technical term for this is the 'wort') is mixed with the yeast, then heated close to boiling point in a tank known as a washback. As the yeast feeds on the sugars in the liquid, it converts them to alcohol and also releases carbon dioxide. This stage takes between 48 and 72 hours, and the result is a rather acidic beer known as the 'wash'.

DISTILLATION

Now the serious business begins: the production of strong alcohol. The wash is run into a still (either a continuous column still or traditional pot still). The principle is the same in either case: bring the wash to a boil to release the alcohol as vapour, which turns back to a liquid as it passes through a condensing coil or 'worm', and from there is channelled off as colourless distillate, known as the 'low wines'. This process is repeated in a spirit still and takes place two (and sometimes three) times.

MATURATION IN CASKS

Before putting the whisky in wooden casks for maturation, water is added to the distillate to reduce the level of alcohol to around 64 per cent alcohol by volume (ABV), which is ideal for the ageing process. The choice of barrel and several other criteria – for example, the type of wood, whether it is a 'first fill' cask or has been used before – all affect how the whisky will turn out.

AGEING

This is where the magic happens. Sheltered in cellars or warehouses and in constant contact with the casks, the colourless distillate slowly transforms into whisky. Maturation time, climatic conditions and geographical location (proximity to the sea is a major factor) form a complex equation that determines how the whisky tastes. To qualify as a whisky, the spirit must have been aged for at least three years. Sometimes maturation includes a 'finishing' process, where the whisky is poured into another cask type (such as a wine cask to mellow the taste) before proceeding to the bottling stage.

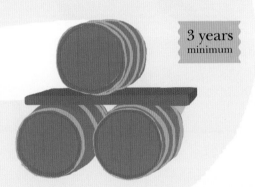

3 years
minimum

BOTTLING

Before bottling, water is again added to the whisky to reduce its alcohol level to between 40–46 per cent ABV. The only exception to this is 'cask-strength' whisky, which is bottled directly from the cask without further dilution. The whisky is then typically chilled and filtered before bottling to remove any final impurities. The downside of chill-filtering is that it removes some of the flavour, so 'non chill-filtered' whisky avoids this issue. Most distilleries leave bottling to specialist bottling plants, with a few exceptions, such as Glenfiddich or Bruichladdich in Scotland, which have their own facilities.

The seven stages of production

TO PEAT OR NOT TO PEAT?

When we talk about whisky, it's hard to avoid talking about peat.

WHAT IS PEAT?

Peat is basically decaying organic matter. After several million years, and aided by a fresh and humid climate, vegetable matter, such as grass and moss, is transformed into peat.

WHERE IS IT FOUND?

This natural resource is found in fields known as 'peat bogs'. Peat bogs exist throughout the world in arctic, subarctic, temperate and tropical environments. In the same way that you have to dig for oil, you have to dig for peat. Some peat bogs are more than 10,000 years old.

HOW IS IT EXTRACTED?

Today, most peat is mechanically extracted, but it used to be dug up using traditional tools (below), then dried in the open air.

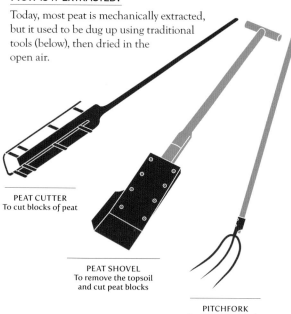

PEAT CUTTER
To cut blocks of peat

PEAT SHOVEL
To remove the topsoil
and cut peat blocks

PITCHFORK
For lifting the blocks
once they are cut

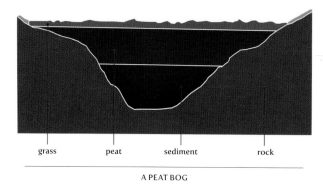

grass   peat   sediment   rock

A PEAT BOG

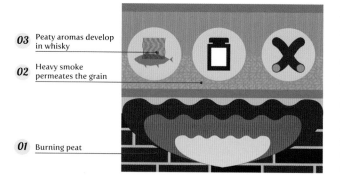

03 Peaty aromas develop in whisky

02 Heavy smoke permeates the grain

01 Burning peat

WHAT IS PEAT'S ROLE IN WHISKY PRODUCTION?

Contrary to popular myth, peat is never soaked in whisky, or rubbed over the inside of casks, but it is used when drying barley during the malting stage. It is set alight and, as it burns, the peat releases a dense smoke that impregnates the malt. The trick is to dry the malt slowly, so that it has plenty of time to absorb the distinctive peaty aroma.

Historically, peat was used as a fuel, so in the past every whisky was peated. Non-peated whiskies were created simply by using a different fuel, such as coal or gas.

In a tasting, a peated whisky does not simply give off a 'peaty' aroma. Instead, it may produce a wide range of aromatic compounds, such as medicinal notes, liquorice, wood smoke, or even smoked fish.

Octomore 6.3:
258 PPM

Ardbeg Supernova:
100 PPM

Highly peated:
higher than 30 PPM
Ardbeg: 50 PPM

Medium-peated:
15–30 PPM

Unpeated whisky:
fewer than 3 PPM
(imperceptible)

THE PEAT SCALE

To find out whether a whisky has been peated a little, a lot, or to infinity and beyond, it is necessary to measure the concentration of phenols, or aromatic compounds, in parts per million (PPM). In other words, how many phenol molecules are present in a sample of one million molecules.

A PHENOL
MOLECULE

How do we know?

Unless you happen to have your own portable laboratory, you won't be able to tell the exact PPM phenol measure, because is never shown on a whisky label. The best bet is to taste it for yourself. Oddly, a whisky of 30 PPM can sometimes seem more peaty than one with 45 PPM. Everything comes down to individual perception in the end.

An endangered species

Peat is being used up much faster than it is being created, and it is so threatened that campaigns have been launched to try to protect it – for example, in the UK, gardeners are encouraged to use peat-free compost. Peat accumulates at a rate of just 1mm (¹/₂₅in) every year, while an average of 20mm (¾in) is stripped away annually.

1 shovelful
= 20 years of peat

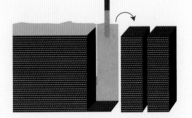

The most heavily peated whiskey

Bruichladdich's Octomore is the peatiest whisky of them all, with an incredible 258 PPM for its Octomore 6.3 Islay Barley expression. Master distiller Jim McEwan achieved this by using a range of innovations both in the blending and ageing processes of the whiskies involved. The result is quite astonishing.

MALTING

Once harvested, the barley must be cleaned of any impurities; the aim of malting is to extract the starch from each cereal grain. Four distinct operations are required before the barley is ready for the distillery.

STEEPING

The barley is soaked in tanks of water for at least two or three days.

DRYING

After around six days, the grains are transferred to a drying kiln, and spread out on a finely perforated floor that has a heat source beneath, in a building often covered by a pagoda-like chimney. Drying is achieved via coal or peat fires, or from air heated to 70°C (158°F), to suspend any additional germination. The length of drying time has a direct impact on the aromas and flavours that develop within the final product. Once it has been dried, the malt can be preserved for several weeks.

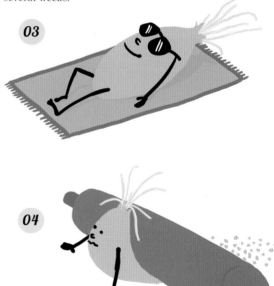

GERMINATION

The barley is then spread out on the malting floor (in a fairly dark but well-ventilated space) to a thickness of around 30cm (12in). Traditionally, maltmen turned the grain by hand with wooden rakes or shovels every eight hours, in a process known as drum malting, but this process is often automated nowadays. Germination is stopped once the germs have swollen to 2–3mm (¾–1in).

GRINDING

This final stage crushes the malt grains into a coarse meal known as grist.

WHICH GRAINS CAN BE MALTED?

Many people think that barley is the only suitable grain for malting. In fact, wheat, corn, rice, rye and oats can all be malted.

TRADITIONAL VS INDUSTRIAL MALTING

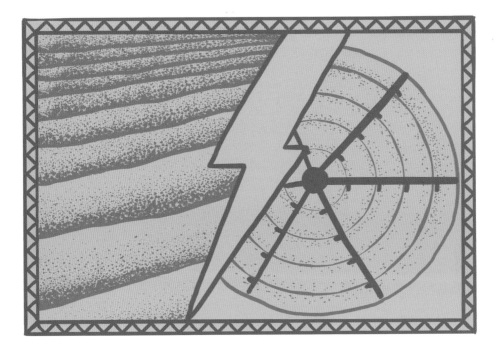

IN INDUSTRIAL DRUM MALTING, THERE IS NO NEED FOR MANUAL RAKING, AS THE BARLEY IS TURNED
BY A SYSTEM OF ROTATING PADDLES

These days, industrial malting has superseded traditional methods, and distilleries tend to outsource the process to specialist malting facilities, for both practical and economic reasons. Those who continue malting in-house do so in limited volumes (perhaps ten to thirty per cent), generally for historical reasons or to attract tourism to the site. The expert view is that drum malting is preferable, creating a better standard of malt that is more homogeneous – even if the process is less attractive to watch.

THE LEGEND OF MONKEY SHOULDER

What have monkeys to do with whisky? To find out, you have to travel back in time and head to Dufftown, on the banks of Scotland's Fiddich River. The town, situated about halfway between Inverness and Aberdeen, still likes to call itself 'The Whisky Capital of the World' – a title it adopted in reference to its nine distilleries – six of which, including the famous Glenfiddich, still operate today. Yet Dufftown was known for another reason: part of its population was struck by a strange malady known as 'monkey shoulder,' a type of arthritis that affected distillery workers, the result of hours spent turning barley with rakes and shovels in the maltings. It is not uncommon in Dufftown to find a retired maltman who still suffers from the condition, the legacy of a time when machines had not yet replaced people for such arduous tasks. Inspired by the maltmen of old, Dufftown's William Grant Distillery produces a whisky that is named Monkey Shoulder.

BREWING

*Before delving any further into the whisky-making process, let us take
a quick detour into the beer brewing process. You'll see why in a moment.*

WHAT IS BEER?

These days, everyone seems to be making beer: your friends, the bar down the street or maybe even your father-in-law. Is it as easy as falling off a log? Maybe – but maybe not. To find out, take just four basic ingredients – water, barley, hops and yeast – and don your apron!

G | THE WORLD'S FIRST BEER

The earliest records of beer production go as far back as the 6th century BC in Mesopotamia. Beer was known as sikaru, but was less of a drink and more of the basis for each daily meal.

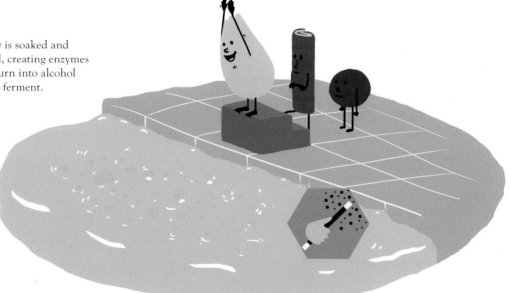

01 **MALTING**
The barley is soaked and then dried, creating enzymes that will turn into alcohol when they ferment.

02 **BREWING**
The malt is coarsely ground, water is added, then the mixture is heated.

03 **HOPPING**
Hops are added, along with spices, and the mixture is brought to the boil. This key stage will give the beer its distinctive smell and taste.

04 **FERMENTATION**
Yeast is added to create alcohol. That's all there is to it!

BREWING IN THE WHISKY-MAKING PROCESS

How does beer relate to whisky?

While it's all well and good to talk about beer, this happens to be, as you know, a book about whisky. But in whisky-making, the brewing stage is more or less identical to that of beer, except for omitting the hops. The resulting 'beer' is then distilled to create whisky. There is, however, one big difference: at no stage is the wort (the water and sugars) boiled. Thus, while yeast converts sugars to alcohol, a number of other important reactions also take place.

How does it work?

The brewing process converts starch in the barley into sugars that can be fermented – and therefore produce alcohol. It all happens in the mash tun (the brewing tank), where grist from the malting stage is mixed with hot water.

Warning: watch the temperature!

If the water gets any hotter than 65°C (149°F), the enzymes in the malt will die – and, along with them, part of the eventual aroma in the whisky. So, if the water becomes too hot, the whisky could have a lot less taste.

 | In brief

Put very simply, whisky is the result of a brewing process (but without hops) followed by a distillation process.

So you could say that whisky is distilled beer!

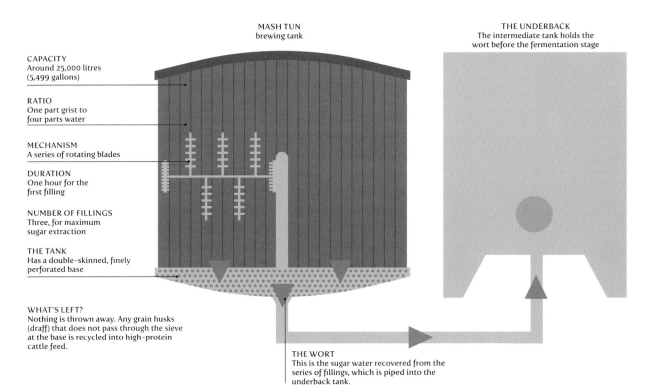

MASH TUN
brewing tank

THE UNDERBACK
The intermediate tank holds the wort before the fermentation stage

CAPACITY
Around 25,000 litres (5,499 gallons)

RATIO
One part grist to four parts water

MECHANISM
A series of rotating blades

DURATION
One hour for the first filling

NUMBER OF FILLINGS
Three, for maximum sugar extraction

THE TANK
Has a double-skinned, finely perforated base

WHAT'S LEFT?
Nothing is thrown away. Any grain husks (draff) that does not pass through the sieve at the base is recycled into high-protein cattle feed.

THE WORT
This is the sugar water recovered from the series of fillings, which is piped into the underback tank.

FERMENTATION

Because it relies on the invisible action of what is basically fungus, the fermentation process is probably the least glamourous part of whisky production. But it is highly technical and essential knowledge, as this is where the alcohol is created.

THE WASHBACK

The washback is the tank where fermentation takes place, creating the first traces of alcohol in the whisky. Washbacks are generally very big, around 6m (20ft) high and 4m (13ft) in diameter. When seen in a distillery their depth is less evident, as the distillery floor is elevated above the washbacks.

WHAT IS FERMENTATION?

In simple terms, fermentation is the chemical transformation of sugar into alcohol by yeasts. Pasteur discovered the process in 1857.

MATERIALS
Traditional washbacks are made from pine or larch. Modern versions are built from stainless steel, which is easier to maintain.

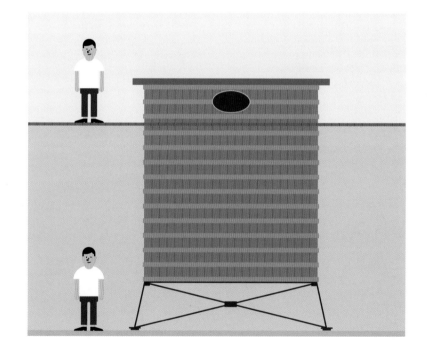

 GEORGES' FAST FACT

The washbacks of the Highland Park distillery in Scotland were used as communal baths for the naval base at Scapa Flow during the Second World War.

 GEORGES SAYS: KEEP YOUR HEAD DOWN!

If you are on a distillery visit and feel tempted to put your head over the washback while fermentation is in progress, you might be in for a surprise. It is an experience that will, quite literally, take your breath away, as a strong whiff of carbon dioxide shoots right up your nose, creating a very unpleasant sensation. Your tour guide may well have a good laugh, though.

YEAST

Yeast belongs to the mushroom family, but its role in whisky cannot be understated. If your favourite whisky has an aroma you particularly like, it could well be down to the kind of yeast that has been used to make it. This is because the fermentation process is the point where esters appear, chemical compounds which in turn give whisky its particular aromas. There are two types of yeasts:

WILD YEAST
Has a very rich aromatic palette, but can also be a source of unpleasant surprises.

CULTURED YEAST
Considered more stable and therefore more widely used. Some distilleries even create their own yeast strains, although these are rare exceptions.

ALL ABOUT ESTERS

In chemistry, an ester is a particular kind of chemical compound, and they are important in the whisky-making process because of their distinctive range of odours. For example, benzyl acetate, which chemists know as $C9H1002$ or $CH3-CO-O-CH2-C6H5$, provides notes of jasmine, pear or strawberry. More than 90 different esters have already been identified in various types of whisky. Ethyl acetate is the one found in greatest amounts, and it is this that gives whisky its characteristically fruity aroma. Esters can appear as early as during the fermentation stage.

THE PROCESS

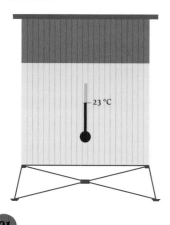

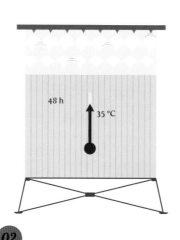

01

The washback is filled to two-thirds capacity with the wort (the sugar water) from the mash tun, which has been cooled to 23°C (73°F). Yeast is added and the process begins.

02

Fermentation lasts up to 48 hours. After adding the yeast, nothing seems to happen at first; then the reaction takes off. Foam forms on the surface and the liquid emits a clicking noise. The temperature of the liquid rises to more than 35°C (95°F).

03

A rotating arm skims off the foam before it can spill over the sides of the washback. In the most extreme cases, the whole massive washback can start to vibrate.

04 Once the fermentation is complete, the acidic beer that is left behind (known as the wash) contains around eight per cent alcohol. It is pumped out and piped to the still for the first distillation.

DISTILLATION

◇◇

Putting a dash of water into your whisky is fine. But in the course of whisky production, water needs to be completely removed, leaving only alcohol behind. That is what distillation is all about. There are various techniques, from two- or three-stage distillation, to 'continuous' distillation. It can even be done in a vacuum.

THE PRINCIPLE

Here comes the science bit, but don't panic: it's actually pretty simple. Distillation is basically a way to separate liquids that have different evaporation temperatures. So it doesn't 'transform' anything into anything else, but simply separates elements from each other. Once heated, different substances vaporize at different times. The vapour is then cooled and condensed back into a liquid, creating the distillate. Water evaporates at 100°C (212°F), alcohol at just 80°C (176°F). The trick is finding the right temperature, slightly higher than 80°C (176°F), to get only the desired chemical substances that, in turn, will impart a distinctive taste to the distillate. Obviously, it is way more complicated than this in an actual distillery because there are dozens of parameters, such as pressure, volume and so on, that have to be kept in check. But you get the idea.

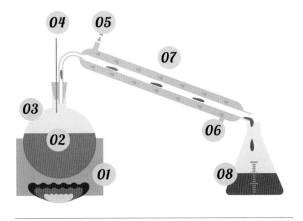

01 The burner heats up the mixture to be distilled.	**05** Outlet for refrigerant.
02 The mixture is heated just to boiling point.	**06** Inlet for refrigerant.
03 The flask in which the mixture is heated.	**07** The condensing tube, whose external walls are surrounded by refrigerant water.
04 A thermometer allows for temperature control during distillation.	**08** The liquid obtained by the process is called the distillate.

A BIT OF CHEMISTRY
Distillation is based on the principle of matter changing states (from solid to liquid to gas), which can be achieved by heating followed by cooling. The material to be distilled is heated in a flask and brought to the boil. Vapour rises to the top, then enters a collection tube, where it is cooled by a refrigerant and returns to its liquid state.

A RISKY BUSINESS?

Distillation requires constant monitoring by a stillman, the specialist who runs the distillation process, aided by an increasing number of automated security systems designed to reduce the risk of accidents. In the past, distilleries were dangerous places, often subject to fires and explosions.

A SHORT HISTORY OF DISTILLATION

Distillation was discovered thousands of years ago. In ancient times, however, the process was used mainly to create essential oils and perfumes. Aristotle was the first to describe the distillation of seawater.

As early as the 8th century, the Arab world had perfected the use of the still to create alcohol, and in the Middle Ages in Europe, distillation came into its own for medicine and alchemy. Distilling alcohol only became widespread in Europe around the 15th century.

TWO-STAGE DISTILLATION

This method is used by the majority of whisky producers to create single-malt whisky. It consists of two successive distillations of the wash from the brewing stage (except in Ireland and a few exceptions in Scotland, such as Auchentoshan, where triple distillations are the norm) using a pair of connected stills: the wash still and the spirit still.

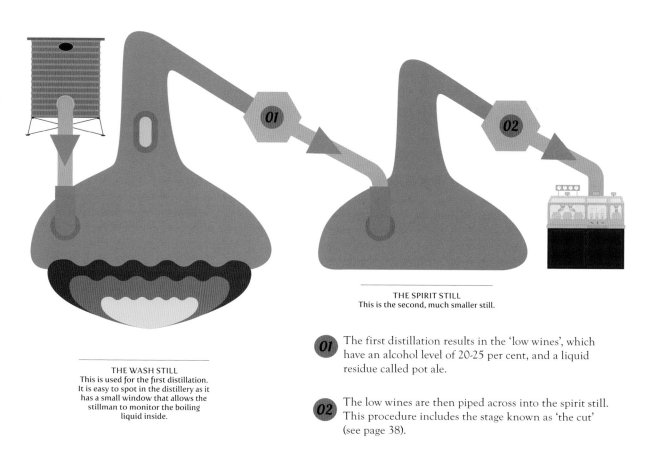

THE SPIRIT STILL
This is the second, much smaller still.

THE WASH STILL
This is used for the first distillation. It is easy to spot in the distillery as it has a small window that allows the stillman to monitor the boiling liquid inside.

01 The first distillation results in the 'low wines', which have an alcohol level of 20-25 per cent, and a liquid residue called pot ale.

02 The low wines are then piped across into the spirit still. This procedure includes the stage known as 'the cut' (see page 38).

VACUUM OR REDUCED-PRESSURE DISTILLATION

Although little-used, this technique is more energy efficient and puts less stress on the stills. At a normal atmospheric pressure, water will boil at 100°C (212°F). The lower the atmospheric pressure, the lower the boiling point, so the less energy required in distillation.

SOAPING THE STILL

To speed up the heating process, some distilleries add an odourless soap during the first distillation to reduce surface tension and thus prevent the liquid from boiling over. This allows the still to be heated more intensively.

CONTINUOUS DISTILLATION

This technique is used mainly to make grain whisky, which accounts for the vast majority of world whisky production.

In this process, distillation takes place in one single, uninterrupted pass.

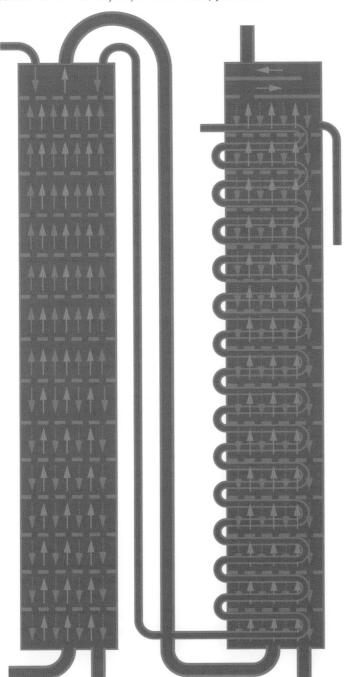

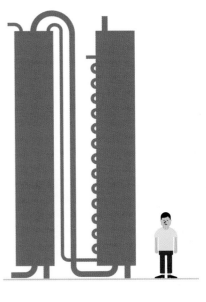

THE COLUMN STILL

Continuous distillation requires the use of a column or Coffey still, named after its inventor. The still works continuously, and produces a highly pure distillate, which can be close to 100 per cent ABV.

 DISTILLATION'S LEFTOVERS

In the distillation process, hardly anything gets thrown away. On the Isle of Islay, waste residues from distilleries have been recycled into bio-gas, used to power electricity generators. In a more extreme example, Scottish scientists have been trialling the use of distillery waste for nuclear decontamination at the nuclear research centre in Dounreay in the far north of the country.

AENEAS COFFEY
(1780–1852)

**His name may sound like a popular hot beverage,
but this man revolutionized the world of whisky.**

orn around 1780, Coffey was an Irishman who began his career as a customs officer, rising quickly through the ranks to become an Inspector General of Excise. His job brought him into close contact with manufacturers of alcoholic beverages, and he became expert in distilling technology, eventually buying his own distillery in Dublin in 1924. It was here that Coffey invented (or more accurately, perfected) a new type of vertical-column still that later bore his name.

Coffey started out with a column still designed by Scotsman Robert Stein, but developed and patented some significant modifications that allowed for the continuous distillation of grains such as wheat and corn, with a resulting liquor that tasted less bitter than that produced from traditional pot stills. What's more, the still required less maintenance and was cheaper to run. He applied for a patent for his design in 1830.

Coffey's countrymen, however, remained unconvinced, and his invention had little traction in its home market. In Scotland, however, the Coffey still proved popular, and the cheaper, easily drinkable whisky that it produced quickly helped Scotch whisky begin to dominate at the expense of Irish whiskey.

By 1835, there was such demand that Coffey closed his distillery and focussed entirely on manufacturing his stills. He created Aeneas Coffey & Sons, a company that specialized in the fabrication of the Coffey still – by this time, also known as the 'patent still'. The firm is still trading today, although under the name of John Dore & Co Ltd.

THE CUT

$\diamond\diamond\diamond\diamond\diamond\diamond\diamond\diamond\diamond\diamond\diamond\diamond\diamond\diamond\diamond\diamond\diamond$

The cut relies on the expertise of the stillman, who has overall control of the distillation process. The challenge is to take the low wines collected from the first stage and separate them into three distinct liquids.

THE 3 STAGES

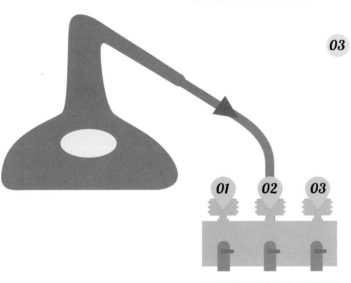

03

THE FEINTS (OR TAILS)

This is the final part of the cut, with a strength of 60 per cent ABV or less, and can be detected by taking a sample and adding water, at which point it will turn blue. The feints are rich in sulphides and pungent aromatics, and are once again redirected into the low wines receiver for distillation a second time.

01

THE FORESHOTS (OR HEADS)

This is the first liquid to arrive at the end of the condenser and it is completely unfit for consumption, as it could cause blindness or even death – that is, if someone still wanted to try it after inhaling its nauseating smell. The foreshots comprises methanol-rich compounds such as ethyl acetates and pungent volatile esters, all of which evaporate at relatively low temperatures and hence are the first to emerge in the distillate. These have an aggressive taste and aroma, and an ABV of around 72–80 per cent. Unsurprisingly, they are always channelled back into the next batch of incoming low wines. The foreshots eventually form catalytic reactions with the copper of the still to add taste and aroma in the whisky. This operation takes up to half an hour, depending on the size of the still.

02

THE MIDDLE CUT (OR HEART)

This is the liquid that the stillman, at a precise moment during the distillation, channels into the spirit receiver, and it is the distillate that will form the basis of the whisky three years down the line. The level is between 68–72 per cent ABV, and the distillation time depends on the quality of whisky required. A slow process leads to a mellower whisky. A faster distillation creates a more aggressive, sulphurous taste.

THE SPIRIT SAFE

A BIT OF HISTORY

A veritable museum piece, the spirit safe is an imposing and beautiful device made of copper and glass that serves as a kind of quality-control laboratory for the distillate from the spirit still. Originally designed to control fraud, the spirit safe measures the exact quantities of liquid emerging from the still, while at the same time preventing the distillery from diverting any liquor from the manufacturing process to avoid paying duties on it. These days, as well as providing a must-see element on any distillery tour, the spirit safe provides a traditional means of testing the distillate in 'real time' to separate the foreshots and feints from the middle cut. Before 1983, only customs and excise officers had access to the spirit safe. These days, every distillery has its own set of keys.

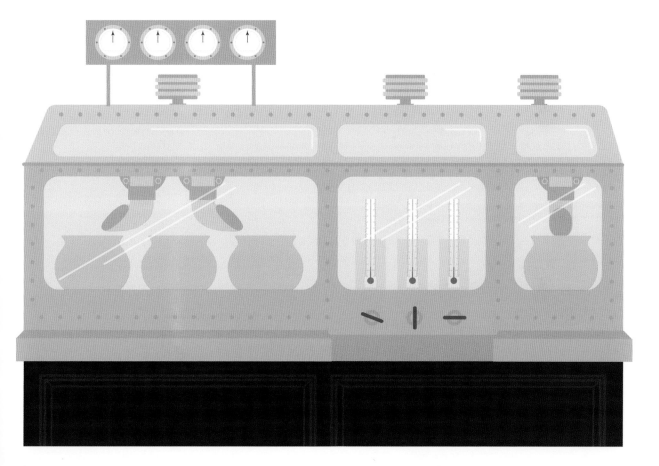

HOW IT WORKS

Imagine NASA's Mission Control at Houston, with its ranks of monitors checking every conceivable parameter. The spirit safe uses basically the same idea, but without the computers and without the rocket science. It is essentially a laboratory locked behind glass, where distillate is tested with a hydrometer to check the alcohol level, and distillate can be run into flasks and mixed with water to check the reaction: milky for foreshots, blue for the feints. Depending on the test results, the stillman directs the distillate either to the spirit receiver, or back to the spirit still.

The cut

BARREL-AGEING

The cask is like a mother to the spirit it holds, playing a decisive role in the evolution of a whisky, protecting it from the elements, and influencing both its colour and also its taste and aroma.

WHY USE CASKS?

While the first evidence of barrels being used for transporting alcohol date from the 15th century, the earliest written records on the importance of maturing alcohol in wooden barrels do not appear until 1818. Increased demand for whisky in both the UK and the USA meant that distilleries were forced to use whatever barrels were available to them at the dock, whether these were originally used for rum, wine or sherry. It is thanks to this necessity, however, that whisky producers began to realize how the choice of barrel heavily influences a whisky's development.

OAK

Oak is the most widely used timber in cask-making, not only because it is readily available, but also because of its particular qualities in the maturation process of whisky.

Two types of oak are most commonly used (and a third more rarely):

- White oak, originally from the USA. Today, around 90 per cent of the casks used in whisky production are made of American oak.

- European oak, which has a softer grain than American oak. This helps create fuller, more intense aromas in the whisky. European oak casks usually had a former life containing sherry.

- A third kind of cask is used in Japan, made from mizunara oak. This wood is very high in vanillins, but also soft and porous, making mizunara casks easily fragile and vulnerable to leakage.

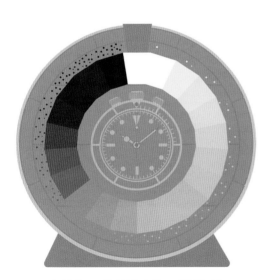

A WHISKY COLOUR WHEEL
The depth of a whisky's colour depends on the type of cask used and the length of time spent in the barrel.

HOW IS THE CASK FILLED?

Casks are filled with the same 'pistol'-style nozzle you would see in a petrol station, but with a wider fuel hose to speed up the process. Once the barrel is full, the cap or bung is replaced and hammered down firmly with a mallet.

WHERE DOES THE COLOUR COME FROM?

The cask is also what imparts colour to whisky during the first years of ageing. The alcohol that enters the cask is clear, but the whisky drawn out at the end of the maturation process has a magnificent hue, ranging from the pale yellow through to deep brown.

THE AROMAS ASSOCIATED WITH EACH KIND OF WOOD

The barrel plays a decisive role in determing the final taste of a whisky.
Some say it influences up to 90 per cent of a whisky's aroma.

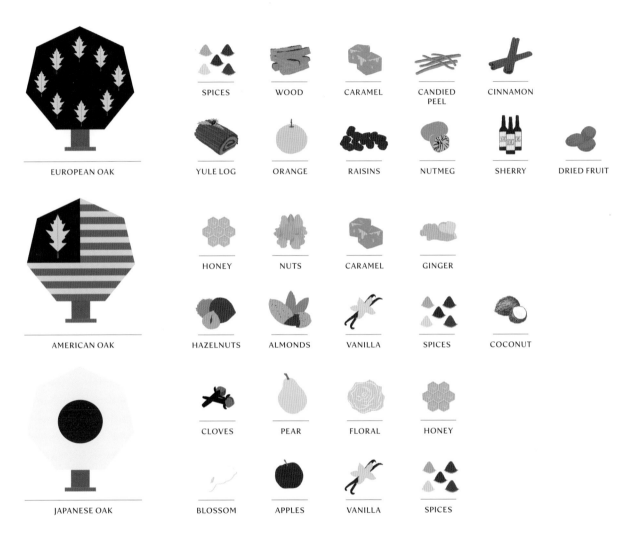

EUROPEAN OAK — SPICES, WOOD, CARAMEL, CANDIED PEEL, CINNAMON, YULE LOG, ORANGE, RAISINS, NUTMEG, SHERRY, DRIED FRUIT

AMERICAN OAK — HONEY, NUTS, CARAMEL, GINGER, HAZELNUTS, ALMONDS, VANILLA, SPICES, COCONUT

JAPANESE OAK — CLOVES, PEAR, FLORAL, HONEY, BLOSSOM, APPLES, VANILLA, SPICES

VARIOUS AROMATIC PROFILES

Whisky aromas derive from a chemical reaction between the distillate in the cask and the many different compounds within the wood, including lignins, tannins, lactones, glycerol and fatty acids. The time spent in cask is also crucial. One of the first reactions occurs with lignins, which produce the organic compound vanillin – this is precisely why bourbons and others of the younger whiskies often have notes of vanilla. Conversely, lactones take much longer to influence maturing whisky; it can take up to 20 years, for example, for a faint note of coconut to be discernible.

SEASONING WITH WINE

To increase aromatic qualities in whisky, distilleries sometimes send casks to Spanish sherry producers to be filled with wine for six to eighteen months. The casks are then returned to the whisky distillers to mature whisky.

HOW ARE CASKS MADE?

Cooperage, or cask-making, is an art form, requiring expert craft skills developed over years of training. It generally takes five years for a novice cooper to acquire the necessary skills: proof, yet again, that when it comes to whisky, nothing can be rushed.

A TIME-HONOURED SKILL

For hundreds of years, all kinds of food and drink have been stored and transported in barrels, so the art of making barrels (or casks) is an ancient one. Despite all the technology available today, the process of cask-making hardly changed over the centuries. The best casks are still those that are made by hand by a highly skilled and qualified cooper.

THE BIGGEST COOPERAGE IN THE WORLD

This is the Brown-Forman Cooperage in the USA, which is owned by the same group that owns Jack Daniel's. It can produce up to 1,500 barrels per day.

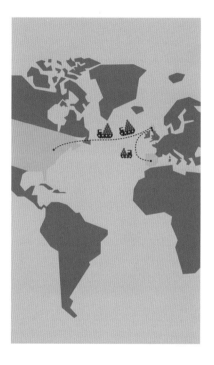

WHY ARE THERE SO MANY BOURBON BARRELS?

During the 1930s, sherry barrels became scarce as production was disrupted by the Spanish Civil War. As a result, Scottish distillers called on the United States to supply them with used bourbon casks. This suited everyone: the US found somewhere to sell its used bourbon barrels (because by law, bourbon has to be matured in new barrels), while Scottish producers found a new source for ageing their whisky. These days, in the average whisky cellar, bourbon barrels outnumber sherry barrels by a ratio of twenty to one.

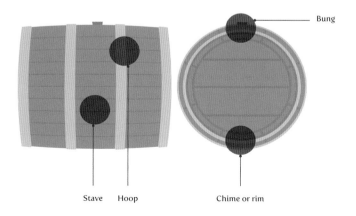

Bung

Stave   Hoop

Chime or rim

WHY THIS PARTICULAR SHAPE?

How is it that a liquid can be contained in a wooden cask without leaking? The answer lies in the shape of the cask, which allows iron hoops to be placed either side of its widest point, keeping the staves (the wooden sections) held very tightly together. The other advantage is that, with a bit of training, the barrel is very easy to manoeuvre, even when full, and can be stored either vertically or horizontally.

THE STAGES OF CASK-MAKING

01

The first, most crucial stage is the selection of timber. Each year, when the new season's trees come into the sawmill, the coopers arrive to select the best oak for their barrels, well aware that this choice will have a direct effect on the quality of the casks produced. The oak is scrutinized before and after it is cut, and the wood is selected according to many factors, including the shape of the original tree and its growing conditions. All this has a bearing on the texture of the wood fibres, the fineness of the woodgrain and the level of tannins in the timber.

TOASTED VS CHARRED

The sherry casks used for whiskey are only lightly toasted whereas bourbon casks are completely charred. The carbonized wood ends up acting like an activated carbon filter, which can help eliminate sulfur compounds to produce a smoother drink. It also gives whiskey a deeper colour and smokey notes of caramel and honey with spicy accents. The charred barrels are then filled with bourbon and left to age for several years. Once they have been emptied, they can no longer be used for the ageing process and they usually continue their life in Scottish or Irish distilleries. The life of a cask varies from 50 to 60 years, after which it is recycled.

02

The logs have to be split by hand to preserve the grain of the wood without breaking the fibres, which is essential for creating watertight barrels. After it is split and planed, the wood is left outside to season for a number of years, during which time it is monitored for the development of sugars and acids.

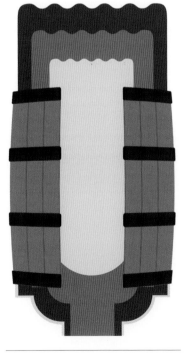

NEW CASKS FOR BOURBON
American casks for bourbon must (by law) be new, and charred in the interior to a depth of around 5mm ($\frac{1}{5}$in).

03

Following this ageing process, the staves are cut by machines. Once cut to the correct length, the ends are tapered and bevelled, and then the staves are planed on the outside surface, with a slight concave profile added to the interior face. Precision machining of the sides ensures that they fit together perfectly once assembled.

04

Once the staves have been passed for quality control, they go to the cooper for assembly. The cooper selects staves that will work perfectly together to form each barrel. He then assembles the staves inside a temporary metal band that holds them together (a process called 'barrel raising'). Steaming the staves makes them flexible enough to be bent into shape and held by a band at the other end of the barrel.

05

The barrel is then alternately soaked in water and heated in the workshop until it takes its final shape.

06

Finally, the cask is tested for its watertight properties, using hot water at high pressure, which immediately reveals any leakages, traces of moisture or manufacturing defects.

How are casks made?

DIFFERENT TYPES OF CASKS

Below are the main barrel types used to mature and transport whisky.

180–200 LITRES

BOURBON BARREL

The most widely used of all, and sourced from the American whiskey industry. In terms of aroma, it adds notes of vanilla and spices.

478–520 LITRES

SHERRY BUTT

The most expensive and heftiest casks come from Spain. The sherry seasoning lends notes of dried fruits and spices to whisky.

225–250 LITRES

HOGSHEAD

With a few more staves than the bourbon barrel, the hogshead is a large cask with a long history. A traditional unit of measure, it was originally the equivalent of 63 gallons.

41 LITRES

FIRKIN

One of the smallest casks that you'll find in any distillery, the firkin is a rarity these days. Firkins were once used to transport beer, fish...even soap!

MIZUNARA CASK

This came into its own due to supply shortages during the Second World War. Made from Japanese oak, mizunara casks are extremely rare – only around 100 are made each year.

HOW MUCH DOES IT COST?

The cost of the barrels represents between ten and twenty per cent of the cost of whisky production. The current situation (the decline in sherry production and the increased demand for bourbon casks) means that barrel prices have increased considerably in recent years. To give you an idea, a bourbon cask costs between £450 ($560) and £550 ($680) and a sherry cask costs between £650 ($805) and £800 ($995). Some casks exceed £1,500 ($1,850) per unit. For this price, you can understand why they are reused for as long as possible.

THE LIFE CYCLE OF A CASK

How many times is a cask used? Depending on the particular distillery and the aromas required, typically three or four times.

FIRST FILL

So-called 'first fill' casks are the most sought-after by distilleries and whisky drinkers. The term doesn't mean this is the first time the cask has been used, as it has already contained bourbon or sherry. However, this is the first time it will have been filled with single malt Scotch. First-fill casks impart maximum flavours from the wood to the whisky.

CASK FIRST AID

Getting a cask to provide close to 50 years of continuous service may require a bit of maintenance in between fills, notably:
- repairing damaged barrels;
- replacing any damaged staves; and
- transforming bourbon barrels into hogsheads by adding staves

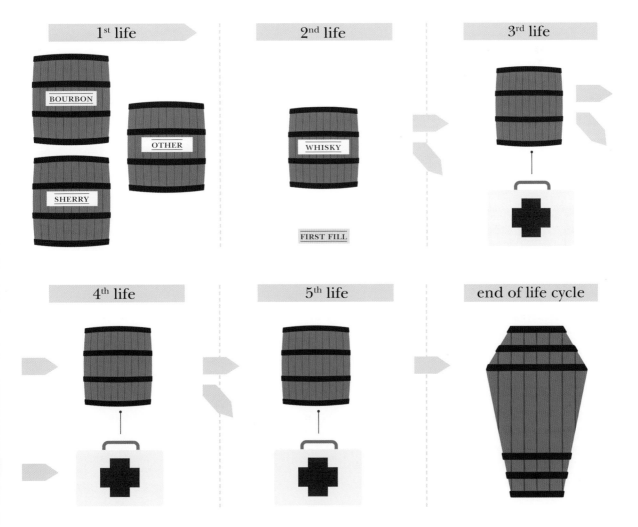

1st life · BOURBON · SHERRY · OTHER

2nd life · WHISKY · FIRST FILL

3rd life

4th life

5th life

end of life cycle

JACK DANIEL
(1849–1911)

If there were ever an enigmatic character in the world of whiskey, then it's Jack Daniel, founder of the eponymous distillery.

Jack Daniel had a tough start to life. His mother died soon after his birth, and his father placed him in the care of a neighbour when he turned six years old. He found refuge with a Lutheran pastor named Dan Call, who also happened to run a distillery. Legend has it that Call taught young Jack about distillation, but Call's still was actually run by a former slave. Nathan 'Nearest' Green was emancipated after the US Civil War, and continued working with Call when he gained his freedom. He was the one who taught young Jack the finer points of the whiskey-making process.

When the pastor gave up distilling, Jack bought the distillery and registered it in 1866, making it the first and the oldest distillery registered in the USA. Green became its first master distiller and the first African American to take such a role. At first, Green and Daniel conditioned their whiskey in regular round bottles; not until 1895 did a bottle-supply salesman suggest square bottles, which today are emblematic of the brand. When you look at a modern bottle of Jack Daniel's, you may wonder why 'Old No. 7' appears on the label. It remains one of those best-kept secrets, contributing to the brand's mystery.

Jack Daniels never married or had children, but engaged one of his nephews to help him with the accounts in his burgeoning distillery. It was he who suggested that Jack put his savings into a strongbox, and only the two of them knew the combination. When Jack forgot the sequence a few years later, he delivered a violent kick to the strongbox and managed to break his toe, an injury that became infected and, the story goes, may have led to his death five years later from blood poisoning.

CHARLES DOIG
(1855–1918)

A brilliant innovator who has left his mark on whisky's heritage, Charles Doig was the man who created the characteristic pagoda roof vents found on dozens of Scotland's distilleries.

Born on a farm in 1855 in the county of Angus, Charles Doig quickly became known for his exceptional intellect, being a frequent winner at the various mental arithmetic competitions that were popular at the time. At age 15 he became assistant to a local architect, who was amazed at Doig's talents, both in geometry and design.

During this period, distilleries in Speyside were expanding to meet growing demand, and Doig was sought out both to design new distilleries, and to renew and enlarge older ones. Many distilleries were prone to accidental fires, and Doig created some innovative solutions, including an early version of a sprinkler system that extended throughout a distillery building.

However, he is best known for his famous 'Doig Ventilator', more commonly called a kiln pagoda. Before then, maltings generally had conical roofs where smoke from buring peat rose through a pointed top. Doig wanted to make them more visually appealing and more efficient at the same time, and pagoda-shaped chimneys achieved this.

The first was built a few kilometres from Aberlour in the town of Dailuaine, and after that, there was no stopping him – or the distillery industry either. Doig is thought to be responsible for no fewer than 56 distillery kiln pagodas.

Because malting is mostly outsourced today, few distilleries still use their kilns, but they remain the lasting face of the Scottish whisky industry.

IN THE WAREHOUSE

Angels take a sip back to heaven, and the elements are invited into the barrel…it is inside a warehouse during the ageing process that the real magic of whisky-making takes place.

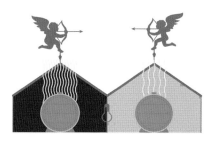

GEORGES INVESTIGATES: THE ANGEL'S SHARE

It's a whimsical term, the angel's share, and it relates to the volume of alcohol that evaporates during the barrel-ageing process. The hotter and dryer the environment, the higher the angel's share becomes. Conversely, a damp and cold environment decreases the amount lost to evaporation.

Playing a key part in the making of any whisky, the warehouse is where the alchemy of the ageing process takes place. But while these warehouses are designed to preserve the whisky (and protect it from theft) they also need to be open to the elements, allowing the distinct local climate to permeate the air inside and leave its mark on the taste of the whisky locked inside the barrels.

BARRELS FROM OTHER DISTILLERIES…

Collaboration is a watchword in the world of whisky distilling, and it is therefore not unusual to see casks from rival distilleries stacked in the same warehouse. There are several possible reasons: the rival distillery may have encountered a technical problem, and the warehouse is lending some temporary space; or the warehouse is in a location that other distilleries believe could be beneficial for their whiskies, and are simply renting some space.

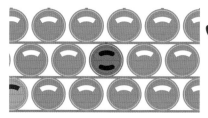

…AND WINE CASKS TOO!

You may find prestigious Bordeaux casks, or specialist dessert wine casks in the whisky warehouse, simply because wine casks, wherever they are from, can add to the aroma of a finished whisky.

GEORGES SAYS: TRY A TASTING

You must try a whisky in a traditional warehouse if you get the chance. Very few distilleries let visitors try a tasting straight from the cask in the warehouse, but some of them will, so it is well worth asking your tour guide. The opportunity to see a cellar master sneak in underneath a barrel and return with a pipette (also known as a 'spirit thief') full of whisky is an experience you'll never forget.

A STROLL THROUGH THE WAREHOUSES

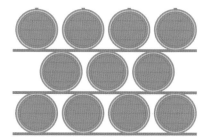

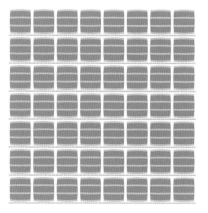

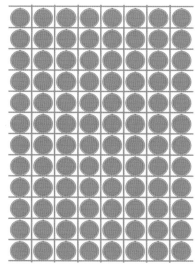

THE TRADITIONAL WAREHOUSE

Scottish distillers are passionate about their 'dunnage' warehouses: low-rise buildings built of traditional stone, with a dirt floor and slate roof. Drafty, dark and damp inside, they are inhabited not only by whisky casks, but also by fungus. And not any old fungus: this is *Baudoinia compniacensis*, which thrives anywhere there are alcohol vapours in the atmosphere, leaving crusts of black fungal growth on the building's stone walls. The advantage of this set-up is mainly that the cool, damp environment limits angel's share losses (due to evaporation) to a low-ish two per cent.

PALLETIZED STORAGE

In these warehouses, casks are stored upright on palettes, which makes for easier access using forklift trucks and reduces overall operating costs. This is all highly efficient, but it's much less appealing to visitors on a distillery tour, who would prefer to be sniffing fungus in a dunnage. It is the most industrialized process of the three.

RACKING WAREHOUSES

Dating from the 1950s, the multi-level racking warehouse is an impressive sight, where visitors feel dwarfed by soaring racks of barrels stacked 12 levels high. The buildings, however, are functional, with a concrete floor to take the weight, and corrugated roofing and block walls. Losses through evaporation are highest at the top of the stack.

WHISKY IN THE CASK IS AFFECTED BY THE ENVIRONMENT OF THE WAREHOUSE

BLENDING

*After the whisky has aged, it is time to begin the blending process
– the final stage before the spirit is bottled.*

A LITTLE HISTORY

Whisky blending was invented in
the mid-19th century, at a time when
the quality of whisky was extremely
variable. Andrew Usher, who worked
for the Glenlivet Distillery during the
1840s, had the bright idea of mixing
several whiskies together to create a
more balanced, harmonious spirit that
was easier to drink. Thus, the blend
was born. Today, blends represent
more than 90 per cent of whisky
sales worldwide.

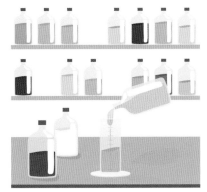

WHY BLENDING?

The art of blending is crucial to the
success of any distillery. Even if every
cask of whisky is filled at the same time,
from the same distillation and in the
same kinds of casks, the resulting whisky
in each cask will be unique, in colour as
well as in taste and alcoholic strength.
Distilleries, however, want every bottle
of a brand to have an identical taste
and appearance. This is where blending
comes in.

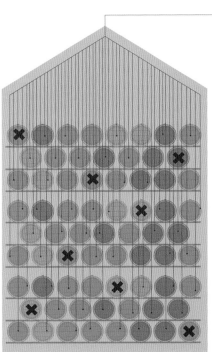

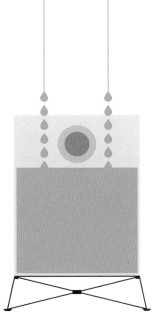

HOW DOES BLENDING WORK?

The master blender selects the casks
that will be used to create the blend
(usually between two and several
hundred). Once the selection is made,
the casks are emptied into a large
stainless-steel tank to create a uniform
result. The blend can sometimes be
subject to additional ageing in casks,
this time over a period of weeks or
months, to ensure a consistent taste
and maximize the aromas.

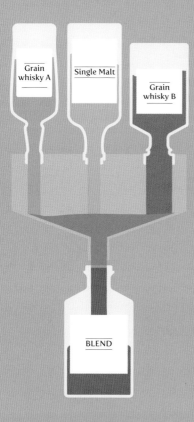

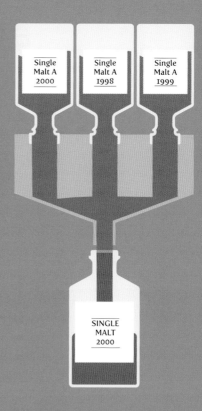

THE BLEND

A blend is a bit like arranging a complex piece of music. Each cask represents a musical note, but the complication is that these musical notes change slightly as the years go on, and there are thousands of them. The master blender has his work cut out: monitoring the evolution of each cask, making sure that the results are as consistent and harmonious as the blends made in previous years.

THE SINGLE MALT

You wouldn't be wrong in thinking that a single malt, unlike a blend, doesn't involve this complex combination process. However, it does involve bringing together the contents of many different casks – all single malts, but from different years and different cask types. The point of this is to create a consistent whisky that does not vary from one year to the next, where the taste and aromas are fairly constant.

Ⓖ THE QUESTION OF AGE

If you buy a bottle of 15-year-old whisky, you might believe that it contains only whisky that has been cask-aged for 15 years. Not so. By law, the bottle must show the age of the *youngest* whisky in the blend. However, most bottles contain additional alcohol that is older, and that adds to the quality of the overall blend. Some whiskies contain alcohol that is twice as old as the age marked on the bottle!

BOTTLING

Bottling is the final link in the whisky-making chain, and the one that provides the connection between the distillery – which has put more than a decade into the process of making the whisky – and the bottle that is sitting in your drinks cabinet. It would be a mistake not to give this final step some well-deserved attention!

DILUTION AND FILTRATION

WHAT'S IT FOR?

Once ageing is complete, whisky has a strength level of around 64 per cent ABV, which is much too strong for your average drinker. It is therefore diluted with water to between 40–46 per cent ABV, using the same type of water that has been used throughout the earlier production stages. Adding this water can, however, precipitate fatty acids, proteins and esters, and leave the whisky looking a little cloudy. To avoid this, the liquid is chill-filtered.

CHILL-FILTERING

Chill-filtering involves cooling the whisky to 0°C (32°F), after which it is passed between cellulose plates to filter out the residues, leaving the liquid perfectly transparent. The downside of doing this is that the whisky can lose part of its aromatic compounds, which are reliant on these residues.

NON-CHILL-FILTERING

To avoid losing flavour during the chill-filtration stage, whisky can still be filtered, but at ambient temperature. Fewer residues are removed, and the strength of such whisky is usually higher than 45 per cent ABV.

CASK STRENGTH

Be prepared for something strong when tasting a cask-strength whisky, as it comes straight from the barrel with no dilution, so can easily have a strength of more than 60 per cent ABV. There is a heady mix of aromas and flavours, too, so it's up to you whether or not to dilute it in your glass in order to appreciate it fully.

G | THE SINGLE CASK

If the label reads 'Single Cask', then the whisky has been bottled from just one unique barrel.

+ You are drinking a whisky that is a very pure reflection of the entire process, from malt to bottle.

– Don't get too attached to what you are drinking, as it will be almost impossible to find another bottle like it. One cask represents only around 100 bottles.

The single-cask phenomenon was originally used only by independent whisky bottlers who differentiated between different brands to seek out the very best casks, but it has since been taken up by most of the big brands.

OFFICIAL BOTTLERS VS INDEPENDENT BOTTLERS

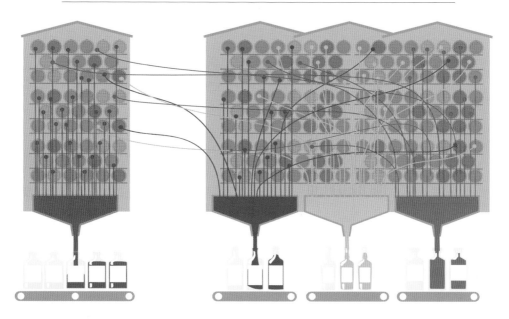

OFFICIAL BOTTLERS

Official, or 'proprietary' bottling simply means that whisky has been bottled by a particular distillery (or its agents), and reflects the specific qualities that the distillery in question has been working to achieve. But whisky is a unique product in that it is also possible to buy casks of whisky from a distillery then bottle it under your own packaging (and marketing). This is precisely what the independent bottlers (or IBs) do. Generally, a distillery sells them casks of whisky that don't reflect the branded house style – which means it is up to the IBs to choose what to do next: give the casks more ageing, or perhaps change the barrels, or use the contents in a blend. Independent bottlers are not obliged to operate in Scotland. Some are based in Belgium, France or Germany, although they generally mark their bottles as 'Distilled in Scotland'.

VINTAGE
Distilled at IMPERIAL Distillery

Speyside Single Malt

Scotch Whisky

- Vintage 1995 -

Age: 20 years
Distilled on: 18.09.1995
Bottled on: 24.09.2015
Matured in: Hogshead
Cask No's: 50222 + 50223
Bottle No.: 336

Due to no chillfiltration, this whisky may turn cloudy when stored in a cool place. It is both more full bodied and full flavoured.

75 cl NATURAL COLOUR 46 % vol.

HOW TO RECOGNIZE A BOTTLE FROM AN INDEPENDENT BOTTLER
Compared with official bottlings, independents such as Signatory Vintage, Douglas Laing or Gordon & McPhail tend to use fairly understated labelling, but pack it with technical information on the whisky.

A WHISKY BOTTLER IN WINE COUNTRY

Michel Couvreur is a Belgian who brought whisky production to France: not the distillation, which remained in Scotland, but the ageing, finishing, blending and bottling. His casks are stored in cellars at Bouze-lès-Beaune – close to the world-famous wine centre of Beaune.

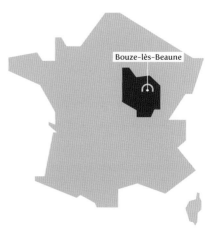

Bouze-lès-Beaune

THE MASTER DISTILLER

*The master distiller is crucial to the continued success of a distillery.
He or (increasingly) she is an almost mythical figure: passionate,
knowledgeable, and possessing an exceptional sense of taste.*

A PATIENT PROFESSION

If you decide to change jobs tomorrow to become a master distiller, then give yourself time – plenty of time. From the day you enter a distillery as a new employee to the moment when you step into the shoes of the master distiller, at least a decade will have passed. Your knowledge will have matured, like a fine whisky, as you engage on a long cycle of testing, learning and understanding. Master distillers work throughout the distillery to gain an in-depth understanding of each stage of the process, but even with all this knowledge and experience under their belt, most remain modest about what they are doing. When it comes to whisky, they will say, it is impossible to understand everything that is going on. Certain qualities are essential: a scientific approach, an excellent nose, a flair for public relations and, of course, a passion for whisky.

WHAT DO YOU TALK ABOUT WITH A MASTER DISTILLER?

Imagine you are on a distillery tour and you find yourself face-to-face with the master distiller. Don't panic. Here are three possible topics to help you through a conversation:
• What type of still do you use in the distillery?
• What was your favourite whisky the last time you were at a tasting?
• On a day like today (indicating the weather outside) what kind of whisky would you suggest drinking?

Generally, you can launch a master distiller onto a subject and they will be able to talk about it for hours and hours: the mark of a true enthusiast.

MASTER DISTILLERS *VS* MASTER BLENDERS

The master distiller is in charge of the distillation process, so is the key player in the creation of single-malt whisky. In the case of blends, however, it is the master blender who holds the crucial expertise. The two positions are thus complementary, but very different indeed.

A DAY WITH A MASTER DISTILLER

Don't imagine that a master distiller spends the whole day in front of a still. His tasks are many and varied, and 24 hours are rarely enough for him to accomplish all of them.

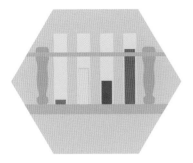

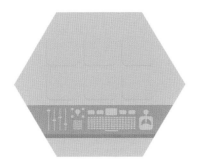

CREATE NEW WHISKIES

No whisky producer can rest on its laurels, and innovation is essential. Even if customers love a traditional house blend, a master distiller is constantly seeking out new products, and uses the distillery laboratory to develop new blends, finishing techniques and more.

MANAGE THE DISTILLERY

The master distiller supervises everything and is responsible for the distillery running to plan 24/7, as well as for finding ways to improve performance.

TEST THE CASKS

Everyone would agree that this is the most pleasurable part of the job. Not a day goes by without the master distiller testing a dram from one of the countless casks. This is purely to understand how far the whisky has got in its evolution, of course!

MARRY THE PAST WITH THE FUTURE

'You don't actually become a master distiller, you simply continue to be one.' That could be the motto of many master distillers who need to understand the history of the distillery thoroughly, while at the same time guiding the brand into the future.

REPRESENT THE BRAND

If you imagined master distillers as retiring types who don't get out much, then think again. You're likely to meet these men and women at various marketing events all over the world, acting as ambassadors for their brands. It is easy to understand why: who better would you select to go out and talk about your product?

The master distiller

OTHER ROLES
IN THE DISTILLERY

The complex nature of a distillery means that there are a wide range of specialist roles that keep it running smoothly. Here are just some of them.

THE STILLMAN
Responsible for the distillation stage, the stillman's jobs include making the 'cut points' that send the middle cut to the spirit receiver, and the foreshots and tails back for redistillation.

THE MASHMAN
The mashman is responsible for the conversion of starch from barley into sugars for fermentation, then the conversion of these sugars into alcohol using yeast in the washbacks.

WAREHOUSE STAFF
Responsible for storage and handling within the warehouse, these workers' tasks include all aspects of filling, draining and racking the casks.

THE DISTILLERY MANAGER

The manager ensures the efficient, safe and secure running of the entire distillery, with responsibility for all the staff – and all the casks.

THE VISITOR CENTRE MANAGER

A distillery is not just a place to make whisky; it is also a tourist attraction. In 2015, more than 1.5 million people visited distilleries in Scotland alone. The role of the visitor centre manager is to create a unique experience for visitors, making sure they safely experience whisky production as it happens, but don't getting in the way of the production process.

 SMALL DISTILLERY VS LARGE DISTILLERY

In the smallest distilleries, you may find the same person doing a number of different jobs (and sometimes all of them!). Edradour, which calls itself the smallest traditional distillery in Scotland, has just three production staff, while Jack Daniel's in Tennessee employs more than 500, all mainly in distillation, bottling and dispatch.

Other roles in the distillery

TOWSER
(1964–1987)

At the entrance to the Glenturret Distillery in Perthshire, Scotland, stands a bronze statue of Towser. During her long life, Towser's ruthless killer instinct led her to claim no fewer than 28,899 victims, all in the name of conserving the quality of the cereals destined for malting. She even made her way into the *Guinness Book of Records*, thanks to the extraordinary number of dead bodies recovered alongside the stills.

Towser, of course, was a cat. If you can excuse the pun, she could also be described as the definitive 'cereal killer'. Legend has it that every evening Towser was permitted a few drops of whisky in her milk, which perhaps explained her gung-ho attitude to mice and her exceptionally long life (for a cat). Such was her fame that the distillery even brought out a bottle of whisky with a picture of Towser on the label.

If Towser was undoubtedly the most famous of all distillery cats, almost all Scottish distilleries like to keep a cat, which can often become something of a mascot for the place. When Towser died in 1987, her place was taken by Amber, who, in contrast to her famous predecessor, didn't manage to catch a single mouse in 22 years!

More recently, Glenturret has been working with the Scottish branch of the Cats Protection charity to recruit for the role of Master Mouser – a national event covered in the national press. And a cat psychologist was even hired to profile the applicants, looking for a cat that would be warm and friendly to the 120,000 annual visitors by day, and a ruthless killer of unsuspecting mice by night.

GOLDEN RULES FOR DISTILLERY VISITORS

A distillery visit can be a good and memorable experience for any whisky-lover. But best get organized first to make the most of it!

PLAN YOUR ROUTE

If travelling to Scotland, you may well be taking a plane, renting a car, and possibly also getting on a ferry. If visiting a distillery on the Isle of Jura, you may well want to take your car on the boat. This all needs careful organization, as ferry timings change with the seasons, and you don't want to be held up on the slipway and miss out on your visit. With distillery visits getting more and more popular, it makes sense to book your accommodation well in advance.

DESIGNATE A DRIVER

Distillery visits usually involve tastings, and tastings involve drinking alcohol. Decide right from the start who is going to be the designated driver on each day, and bear in mind the strict limits on alcohol when driving in Scotland (currently 0.05g per 100ml of blood) which means the safest bet is not to drink and drive at all.

AVOID THE MOST TOURISTY DISTILLERIES

This all depends on your tastes, of course, but some distilleries seem closer to museums than to a living, working distillery that is part of the 21st century. Consider avoiding the largest distilleries and visit the smaller ones. There, you'll be more likely to be able to talk with the staff and sense the real passion that they have for the work.

CAN I BRING BACK BOTTLES IN MY SUITCASE?

This is a good idea, as distilleries will always have limited editions or bottles that are simply unavailable where you live. If travelling home to another country, bear in mind there will be customs limits to how many bottles per person you are permitted to take with you. And in case you were thinking of a way around this, putting bottles in your kids' luggage doesn't work!

DUTY-FREE SALES

Even if you are not visiting distilleries, but find yourself in the UK for other reasons, take time to check out the shelves in the airport or other duty-free shop. Major distilleries often develop brands that are only sold in duty-free outlets, and you may pick up something interesting.

BEWARE: SIZE MATTERS!

People sometimes find their bottles of whisky confiscated at customs because they have more than the legal amount. UK and US customs both limit passengers to 1 litre of alcohol per person, so beware stocking up on more than one large bottle.

N⁻2
TASTING

This whisky-tasting thing: it's difficult, complicated, and full of weird words, right? Think again. With just a little practice, you can enjoy a whole range of tastes and aromas in your glass that you never even realized were there. This is a journey through the senses, with a whisky glass at hand at all times. Ready?

PREPARATION

It is finally time to open some bottles and embark on a whisky tasting.
A bit of preparation will go a long way to making it a success.

WHERE TO TASTE?

You should aim to have the most neutral surroundings possible; this includes having clean air. If you're serious about tasting your whisky, it is better to leave smoking – or vaping – out of the equation. A bit of unobtrusive music would be ideal, as long as it does not get in the way of quiet conversation. The key word here is mellow.

01 INVITE YOUR FRIENDS

Each person has a unique sense of taste, but a tasting is best done with a group: with friends, family or neighbours. Tasting socially like this allows for an exchange of views, for debate and discussion, and for a chance to discover aromas you might otherwise have missed. Choose your group with care, though. Watch out for the experienced whisky taster with a tendency to become a whisky bore, and bear in mind that newcomers to the activity can easily feel left out. It's all a question of balance.

02 THE CHOICE AND ORDER OF THE BOTTLES

You can try any and all whiskies imaginable during a tasting, but you'll need to think about the order in which you do so; otherwise you risk tasting nothing after your second glass.

Some possible themes include:
- the world tour;
- a region (a collection of Speyside distilleries, for example);
- whiskies with different characteristis – a peated one, a bourbon, a blend;
- a 'vertical tasting': whiskies from the same distillery but with different ages, finishes or expressions.

Rules of the order:
- taste from the weakest to the strongest;
- the least peated to the most peated;
- the youngest to the oldest.

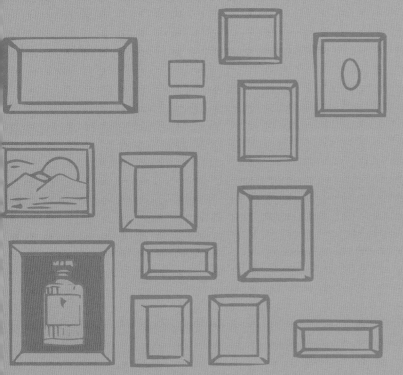

03 FIND YOUR WHISKY YARDSTICK

Your 'whisky yardstick' is your reference whisky: a familiar one that will help you get your bearings at the start. It's useful to begin with this whisky so you can see if it tastes as it normally does. If it doesn't, then it could be that your sense of taste isn't behaving in its usual way, and it might be better to put off the tasting until later.

04 WATER, WATER EVERYWHERE

Make sure you always have plenty of water on the table (ideally Scottish spring water). If there is one thing you are going to drink in big quantities during a tasting, it is water.

05 THE TASTING NOTES

Taking notes on what you taste may look more like work than pleasure, but notes are what allow you to learn as you go, and this will give you even more enjoyment during your next tasting. (For more on notes, see pages 84–86.)

06 THE GRAND FINALE

If you have the chance (and the budget), include a really exceptional bottle at the end of the tasting: an old distillery whose bottles have become a rarity, or a bottling that is little-known, or perhaps a whisky from a specific year. Do your homework, and be ready to go large on all the finer details. It could make for a memorable tasting for everyone present.

REMEMBER TO EAT FIRST

It's a common error among beginners to try tasting on an empty stomach. This is a huge mistake, for many reasons – not least because you're much more susceptible to getting inebriated. Additionally, the first sip of the first whisky will whet your appetite, only making your hunger worse; so will having to think of tasting notes like 'toasted barley', 'vanilla caramel' or 'fruit flavours', which means you won't be able to enjoy the tasting. Eating first also impacts on your ability to taste, as it allows for better concentration, so you can really focus your senses on the task in hand.

ALCOHOL AND THE HUMAN BODY

What happens in the body when we drink alcohol?
Here is a short guide to where it all goes.

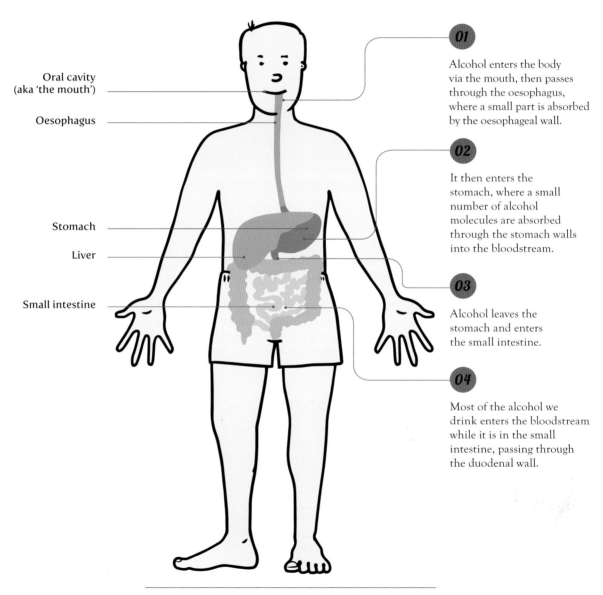

Oral cavity
(aka 'the mouth')

Oesophagus

Stomach

Liver

Small intestine

01

Alcohol enters the body via the mouth, then passes through the oesophagus, where a small part is absorbed by the oesophageal wall.

02

It then enters the stomach, where a small number of alcohol molecules are absorbed through the stomach walls into the bloodstream.

03

Alcohol leaves the stomach and enters the small intestine.

04

Most of the alcohol we drink enters the bloodstream while it is in the small intestine, passing through the duodenal wall.

THE PATH OF ALCOHOL THROUGH THE DIGESTIVE SYSTEM

WHERE NEXT? ALCOHOL IN THE BLOODSTREAM

Alcohol molecules are very small and dissolve easily in water or fats, making it easy for them to diffuse rapidly into all the body's organs.

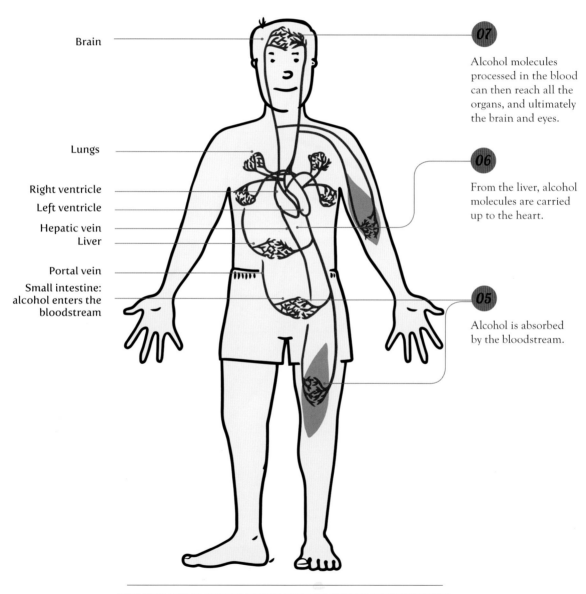

Brain

Lungs

Right ventricle

Left ventricle

Hepatic vein
Liver

Portal vein

Small intestine:
alcohol enters the
bloodstream

07

Alcohol molecules processed in the blood can then reach all the organs, and ultimately the brain and eyes.

06

From the liver, alcohol molecules are carried up to the heart.

05

Alcohol is absorbed by the bloodstream.

THE PATH OF ALCOHOL THROUGH THE CIRCULATORY SYSTEM

Alcohol and the human body

WHAT HAPPENS NEXT?

GETTING IT OUT OF YOUR SYSTEM

People's bodies react very differently to alcohol. The liver can only metabolize a certain amount of alcohol each hour (between 15mg and 17mg), but how fast your own liver can operate depends on your genetic make-up.

WHY IS WHISKY ABSORBED MORE SLOWLY THAN WINE OR BEER?

Whisky contains more than 20 per cent ABV, and alcohol acts as an irritant to the stomach wall, slowing its passage through the pyloric valve, which leads from the stomach to the small intestine. Even drinking a series of whiskies means that the effects of the alcohol won't be felt until later.

THE CONSEQUENCES

Alcohol has an immediate effect on several parts of the body:
- **Heart rate and blood pressure:** in small quantities, alcohol will raise the heart rate and blood pressure; conversely, when drunk to excess, it has the opposite effects.
- **Kidneys:** they have to work harder, which means you will need to urinate more frequently.
- **Skin:** contrary to popular myth, alcohol doesn't raise body temperature. In fact, it is only the skin that gets warmer, while the rest of the body loses heat.
- **Brain:** alcohol affects how the brain functions across several areas, including judgement, reactions and coordination.
- **Hydration:** alcohol also affects a gland that controls the body's hydration, and the body becomes dehydrated, leading to tiredness, neck and back pain, and headaches.

DRINKING ON AN EMPTY STOMACH

If your stomach is empty, alcohol will find its way into the bloodstream more quickly: in as little as half an hour or less. On a full stomach, this would normally take around 90 minutes or longer.

WHAT CAUSES THE HANGOVER

Once in the bloodstream, alcohol spreads quickly into the parts of the body containing water. As the brain contains many blood vessels, it is one of the main targets: hence the classic hangover headaches.

CARRY NATION

(1846–1911)

One determined woman shook up the entire United States whiskey industry, and brought many drinking establishments (and their clientele) to their knees.

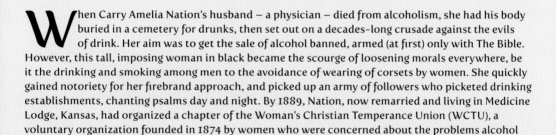

When Carry Amelia Nation's husband – a physician – died from alcoholism, she had his body buried in a cemetery for drunks, then set out on a decades-long crusade against the evils of drink. Her aim was to get the sale of alcohol banned, armed (at first) only with The Bible. However, this tall, imposing woman in black became the scourge of loosening morals everywhere, be it the drinking and smoking among men to the avoidance of wearing of corsets by women. She quickly gained notoriety for her firebrand approach, and picked up an army of followers who picketed drinking establishments, chanting psalms day and night. By 1889, Nation, now remarried and living in Medicine Lodge, Kansas, had organized a chapter of the Woman's Christian Temperance Union (WCTU), a voluntary organization founded in 1874 by women who were concerned about the problems alcohol was causing in their families and communities.

To start with, drinkers found it all a bit of joke, but as time went on, clients began to quit their habitual bars to prevent their names from being published by Nation's group in local newspapers. Sales of alcohol slowed, and barmen ended up putting their liquor out on the road as a sign of defeat.

Carry Nation is best known, however, for her axe-wielding attacks on bars, smashing open casks and pulverizing bottles of liquor. The story goes that it was her second husband who gave her the idea as he teased her about her activities: 'How about using an axe to create even more damage?' he suggested, to which she replied: 'That's the most sensible thing you have said since I married you!' The legend of Carry Nation was born, and the WCTU still flourishes today.

TASTING EXPLAINED

Everyone is different when it comes to tasting and that's exactly what makes whisky-tasting so exciting. Although it can seem daunting and take a little time to learn, learning to taste will increase the enjoyment – and understanding of – the whisky you drink.

WHAT IS A TASTING?

Whisky-tasting is a real pleasure but also a creative activity. It allows people to move out of their comfort zone and experience new things. Think of it as a way of 'recalibrating' your senses of taste and smell and the feelings associated with each of those, in what will eventually become a permanent shift. It is a deeply personal thing, and one of the trickiest aspects can be finding the right words for what you're experiencing – which is why your tasting notes will be different to those of your neighbours. Each tasting, however, tells a story, and by capturing that, you have a permanent record that will be unique to you.

IT'S ALL IN THE BRAIN

Neuroscience and whisky don't sound like the most obvious combination, but that said, researchers for all the major brands spend a great deal of time and money understanding how a drinker experiences a new aroma, or how the packaging, or colour or any other aspect can affect people's perception of a whisky. It's a serious, scientific business.

AN ACQUIRED TASTE

Remember the first time you had a sip of beer or coffee? For many people, that first taste is an unpleasant experience, and this can apply to whisky, too. So how come most people end up liking drinks they started out hating? It all has to do with time and experience, as we accumulate a vast internal taste-memory of styles and tastes, likes and dislikes, and a deepening sense of perception.

 COGNITIVE NEUROSCIENCE: WHAT'S UP WITH THAT?

Cognitive neuroscience is a field of research that studies the neurobiological mechanisms that underpin our cognition. In other words, how our brains make sense of the world around us – including the thousands of types of whisky that inhabit that world. So it is about perception, movement, language, memory, reasoning and even emotions. Researchers draw on the related areas of cognitive psychology, brain mapping and neuropsychology.

A MULTISENSUAL ART

01

'THE NOSE' KNOWS...

Some people, such as Richard 'The Nose' Paterson, can tell which region a Scottish whisky originates from simply by its aroma. And he is not alone in this skill. Through rigorous hours of training, anyone can become highly skilled at this. But it does take an extremely long time.

02

...AND THE EYES HAVE IT

Our sense of smell does not work in isolation, and our overall taste is also influenced by what we see. This is why some big brands put caramel colouring in their whiskies. In the same way, the words we associate with whisky also impact the overall tasting experience.

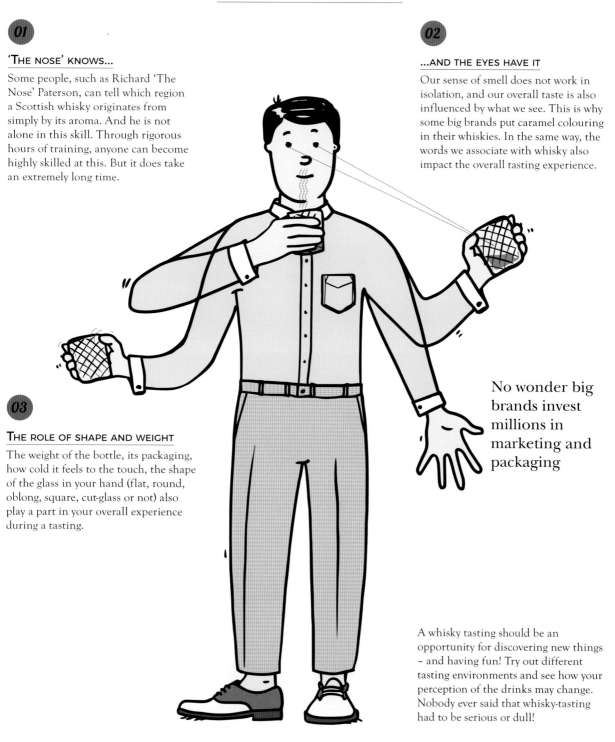

No wonder big brands invest millions in marketing and packaging

03

THE ROLE OF SHAPE AND WEIGHT

The weight of the bottle, its packaging, how cold it feels to the touch, the shape of the glass in your hand (flat, round, oblong, square, cut-glass or not) also play a part in your overall experience during a tasting.

A whisky tasting should be an opportunity for discovering new things – and having fun! Try out different tasting environments and see how your perception of the drinks may change. Nobody ever said that whisky-tasting had to be serious or dull!

THE RIGHT GLASS

Choosing your whisky is one thing. Choosing the right glass to drink it from is even more important. A bad choice at this stage can ruin all your best-laid plans – a bit like wearing trainers to a formal dinner.

THE TUMBLER

Frequently seen as the whisky glass of choice in films and on TV, this is actually not the ideal glass in which to appreciate the aromas of whisky and is best suited for whisky cocktails. They vary in height from the shorter rocks or lowball glass to the taller highball.

THE COPITA

Also called the catavino or snifter, this is easy to mistake for a wine glass, and it is in fact a design that was developed for sherry tastings. Tall and tulip-shaped, it concentrates the aromas in the glass, and the stem keeps your hands (and any unwanted aromas) at a distance.

THE GLENCAIRN

This is a more robust version of the copita, and presents an informal kind of glass designed specifically for whisky-tasting, with a rounded base to liberate the aromas, and a tulip shape to concentrate them at the nose.

HOW THE GLASS INFLUENCES TASTING

Obviously, a glass is for drinking. But it has another function, too: allowing you to pick up all the aromas in the whisky – the activity that the language of tasting calls 'nosing.' A whisky will come across differently, depending on which kind of glass you are using. The glass needs to allow space for your nose to pick up the aromas coming off the surface. But if the glass is too wide, the aromas will be lost almost immediately. A tulip-shaped glass, narrowing at the top, will capture more complexity than a straight glass. Even the texture of the glass plays its part: whisky from a cut glass receptacle can seem different from the same whisky served in a plain glass. So your sense of touch is also involved in the tasting!

So how do I choose?

Try out various glasses, but at the end of the day simply pick the glass that gives you the greatest pleasure to use. There's no point in buying a set of fancy copitas when you'd really prefer an everyday tumbler.

The old fashioned

This version of a tumbler takes its name from the cocktail. Generally made from cut crystal, it was developed in the 1800s for drinking a mixture of whisky with sugar, water and ice: the forerunner of the famous Old Fashioned cocktail.

The quaich

More likely to be found in a museum, antique shop, silversmith or wood-turner's studio than in your local neighbourhood bar, the quaich is a traditional two-handled drinking cup that has been in use in Scotland for hundreds of years. The earliest versions were made in wood, and later editions were produced in silver or pewter.

The watch-glass lid

Specifically designed to contain the aromas until the whisky is ready for nosing, the lid for a tasting glass is often made in the form of a watch glass (a simple concave disc of glass) that sits securely over the rim of the glass. Today these are also available as lids with a small handle, and both kinds of lids (with handles, and watch glasses) are easily obtained from whisky specialists.

 The power of marketing

When whisky is sold in a presentation box containing the bottle and some accompanying glasses, the glasses help to 'sell' the whisky. Some suppliers have pushed the function of the glass even further, such as Ballantine's famous 'Space Glass', which allows you to drink your whisky in zero gravity as you settle in for your next space flight.

 In the interest of transparency

Tinted glass is not an option for whisky-tasting. The look of the whisky influences taste, and it is essential that whisky-tasting glasses are perfectly clean and completely transparent. So best leave those smoke-grey tumblers in the back of the cupboard.

BOTTLE OR DECANTER?

Like the tumbler, the carafe is often a feature of whisky-drinking in films or on TV.
But does it have any real purpose, other than just looking fancy in a drinks cabinet?

DECANTER VS CARAFE

Putting wine into a carafe is not actually the same thing as decanting. Pouring wine into a carafe is all about allowing the wine to aerate, and is often used for younger wines. The action of pouring the wine releases and mixes its constituent parts with oxygen, making it more appealing to drink. Decanting, by contrast, is designed to allow the deposits in an older wine to fall out of suspension.

WHISKY: A FINISHED PRODUCT

Once whisky has been bottled, it is basically finished. In other words, a 12-year-old whisky will remain a 12-year-old whisky even if you leave it in your cellar to 'age' for subsequent years.

NO NEED FOR A CARAFE

There is no need to decant your whisky, as in most cases there will be no deposits (except in the case of non-chill-filtered whisky). And the action of pouring it into a carafe has a limited effect. You may as well simply leave the whisky in your glass. The only possible use of a carafe would be in a blind tasting, where you don't want the label to bias people's opinions or taste.

BUT IF YOU INSIST....

If you really must use a carafe, here are some tips on choosing the right one.

DESIGN
Choose a decanter that you enjoy looking at and that is good at pouring, as the only useful aspect of this thing will be as something pleasing to the eye, that is agreeable to pick up, and pours the whisky effectively into your glass.

IS IT AIRTIGHT?
Check there is a good airtight join at the stopper. It would be a shame to invest in a decanter and then find that it's letting your best whisky evaporate.

CAPACITY
Remember that most whisky is sold in 75cl or 1-litre bottles, so check the capacity of the decanter. Many are smaller than this.

SOME POPULAR DECANTER STYLES

TAYLOR DOUBLE OLD FASHIONED
– RAVENSCROFT CRYSTAL

LEXINGTON

GLOBAL VIEWS

G

LEAD CRYSTAL: THE INVISIBLE MENACE

Congratulations! You have finally found the perfect decanter you've been searching
for, in beautiful crystal. Now you want to get started, decanting one of your most
cherished bottles of whisky. But wait up. The problem with traditional crystal is that
it contains a high lead content, and this can leach into the alcohol. So before using
your decanter you must fill it with a strong alcohol solution for an entire week to
extract a maximum of lead. Even then, you should plan to use your decanter only
to serve whisky, and never to stock your liquor over weeks and months, as the lead
level in the whisky will rise to dangerous levels even after just a few weeks. The best
bet is to choose a decanter made of lead-free crystal.

Bottle or decanter?

WHISKY AND WATER

It is a perennial question in the world of whisky-drinking: should I add water or ice to my whisky? Here is the case for both.

THE IMPORTANCE OF WATER

If the whisky you're drinking is good, one reason for that is the amount of time it has already spent in contact with water during the production process. The first time is during the brewing stage, when the grist is mixed with warm water in the brewing tanks. Also, if your whisky contains 40–46 per cent ABV, it means that before being bottled it was diluted with water to bring the alcohol content down to a more acceptable level.

PUT WATER IN MY WHISKY? NO WAY!

Many old-school purists flatly refuse to add anything to the whisky that flows straight from the bottle, believing that in this way they are drinking whisky in its perfect state as defined by the distillery, with all the aromas and tastes emerging on cue. They'll try to find plenty of ways to convince you of this – although, sadly for them, this view has now become fairly outdated.

WHAT HAPPENS WHEN YOU ADD WATER?

During a whisky-tasting it is always interesting to see what happens when you add a little water. It produces a chemical reaction that reveals much more of the aromas and taste of the whisky, and both nose and taste are transformed. For this reason, whether nosing or tasting, it is always a good idea to try the whisky without water first, then see the difference when water is added.

WHICH WATER WORKS BEST?

If you do opt to add water to your whisky, be as choosy about your water as you would be about the whisky itself. Avoid tap water, as it sometimes has a chlorinated taste, which will change or obliterate whisky aromas. Instead, go for spring water, and if you can, seek out water from the region where the whisky was made – such as Speyside Glenlivet, which is extremely pure and actually used in whisky production. This, of course, is not the easiest water to get hold of, so a good substitute is any good, natural mineral water.

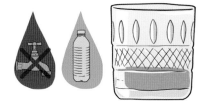

AND IF I PUT ICE IN MY WHISKY?

While adding water opens up the aromas, ice can have the opposite effect, closing down some of the taste. Once again, film and TV series are full of images of whisky being poured into a tumbler full of ice cubes: very photogenic, but with the same result as leaving a good bottle of white wine in the fridge for too long. The whisky will be refreshing and the alcohol burn less evident, but the spirit's complexity will only become evident once it warms up. For blended whiskies and entry-level bourbon, ice tends to have less impact, as they are often designed with this in mind.

HOW MUCH WATER SHOULD I USE?

How long is a piece of string? If there is one thing that remains very ill-defined, it is how much water should be added to a whisky. You could start with just a few drops, and leave it for a while, swirling the whisky in the glass from time to time. Test it, then add a little more, until you really feel you're getting a maximum sense of the aromas and taste. No one has the same nose or palate, so don't be surprised if you need to add twice as much water for a friend to achieve the same results. During professional whisky tastings, experts generally try to dilute the whisky to around 35 per cent: a level that can reveal a large number of aromas.

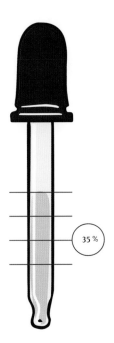

35 %

WHAT ABOUT WHISKY STONES?

For diehard purists who want to drink their whisky cold but don't want to add ice or water, then cooling stones, commonly called whisky stones, are an option. They make an excellent gift, coming (as all stones do) from ancient rocks dating back millions of years. However, if you really want to drink your whisky cold, simply put it in the fridge before serving. It's that simple.

THE THREE STAGES OF WHISKY TASTING

WHAT YOU NEED

1 tasting glass
20ml (4 tsp) of whisky

THE VENUE

Find a place where you feel at home: neither too warm nor too cold, somewhere quiet and cosy where you can settle in for the duration of the tasting. Found it? Then let's get started!

THE TECHNIQUE

Pour the whisky into the glass just before starting the tasting. If it sits in the glass for too long, the most volatile aromas will be hard to spot. Some people place a lid, or watch glass, over the glass once the whisky is poured. It looks good, but has only a limited effect.

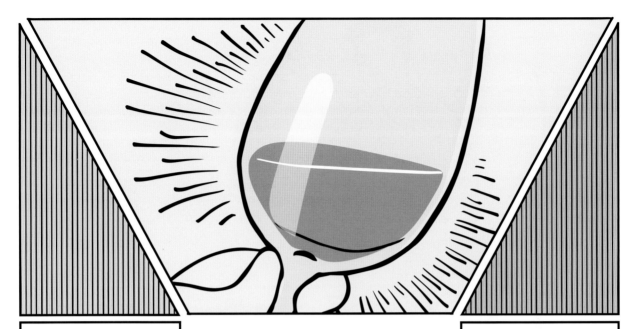

COLOUR

Your first encounter with whisky is a visual one, but don't be fooled by the colour. It's partly due to the cask-ageing process (remember, whisky is transparent when it leaves the still) but it may also be the result of artificial colouring that was added before bottling: a marketing ruse.

APPEARANCE

THE 'LEGS'

Lightly swirl the whisky in your glass and turn it gently to let the liquid coat the sides. Returning the glass to the vertical, watch the 'legs' of whisky drip back down inside the glass. Thin, fast-moving legs indicate a young or light whisky; thick, slow-moving legs mark a heavier, older whisky.

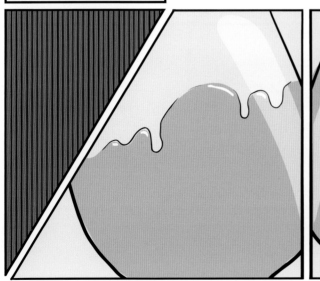

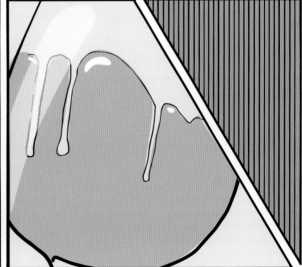

The three stages of whisky tasting

NOSING

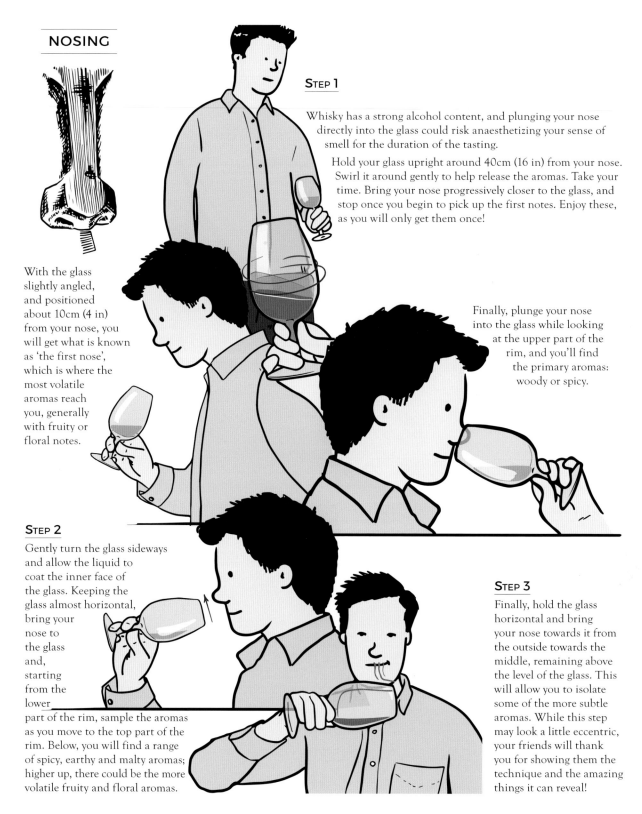

Step 1

Whisky has a strong alcohol content, and plunging your nose directly into the glass could risk anaesthetizing your sense of smell for the duration of the tasting.

Hold your glass upright around 40cm (16 in) from your nose. Swirl it around gently to help release the aromas. Take your time. Bring your nose progressively closer to the glass, and stop once you begin to pick up the first notes. Enjoy these, as you will only get them once!

With the glass slightly angled, and positioned about 10cm (4 in) from your nose, you will get what is known as 'the first nose', which is where the most volatile aromas reach you, generally with fruity or floral notes.

Finally, plunge your nose into the glass while looking at the upper part of the rim, and you'll find the primary aromas: woody or spicy.

Step 2

Gently turn the glass sideways and allow the liquid to coat the inner face of the glass. Keeping the glass almost horizontal, bring your nose to the glass and, starting from the lower part of the rim, sample the aromas as you move to the top part of the rim. Below, you will find a range of spicy, earthy and malty aromas; higher up, there could be the more volatile fruity and floral aromas.

Step 3

Finally, hold the glass horizontal and bring your nose towards it from the outside towards the middle, remaining above the level of the glass. This will allow you to isolate some of the more subtle aromas. While this step may look a little eccentric, your friends will thank you for showing them the technique and the amazing things it can reveal!

TASTING

While nosing, you may have worked up a serious desire to taste the whisky. Be patient, and make sure you don't skip any of the three stages, or you will get a lot less from the overall tasting.

THE FINISH

Finally, pay attention to the finish, which is the length of time you continue to sense the flavours and aromas in your mouth after you have swallowed. The amount of time (short, medium, long) will allow you to describe the whisky's length.

WHEN BEST TO ADD WATER?

Once you've completed the nosing and tasting of the undiluted whisky, add a few drops of water and begin the steps again in the same order. Some of the aromas that previously seemed minimal or absent may now spring to the fore, either in the nose or the mouth. You can repeat this process several times with the aim of finding as many aromas as you can. Make sure, however, not to drown the whisky in too much water. If you find you can no longer differentiate the tastes, then take a break. A breath of fresh air or a glass of cool water will get you back on track.

THE SWIRL

Take a small quantity of whisky to start with, and roll it around your mouth with your tongue, up against your palate, to cover most of the inside of your mouth. At the same time, try to talk as you do this, and allow your tongue to do its work, sensing the difference in taste between the different parts of your mouth.

THE SWALLOW

The action of swallowing creates a phenomenon known as retro-olfaction, which basically means that the whisky aromas arrive in your nose via the back of your oral cavity. If you put your nose to the glass at this moment, you will perceive the aromas in your glass slightly differently. It's like magic!

Finally, remember always to drink water between each whisky in the tasting to cleanse your palate.

 THE ROLE OF THE SALIVARY GLANDS

If you feel your mouth watering while nosing the whisky, or indeed when you taste it, then this is actually a good thing, which will improve your tasting experience. The alcohol in the whisky mixes with your saliva to transform into sugar, and the effect will improve the taste of the whisky, making it feel a little rounder!

 TO SPIT OR NOT TO SPIT?

That, indeed, is the question. Some say it's impossible to taste a whisky properly if you haven't swallowed it, as you miss out on the retro-olfaction stage. However, much of essential tasting happens without swallowing. If you're going to swallow each sample, limit the number of bottles – unless you want to end up under the table before the tasting is over!

The three stages of whisky tasting

THE FLAVOURS OF WHISKY

The world of whisky flavours is a complex one, provoking much debate as well as research and discovery. More than 100 flavours have been officially classified, which makes whisky one of the most wide-ranging aromatic spirits around.

CLASSIFYING AROMAS? IT'S A NIGHTMARE!

Aromas are difficult to pin down. There is no set of standard descriptors for aromas, nor can primary aromas be measured or defined. If this weren't hard enough, it can be complicated by cultural factors. Odours can be perceived, learned and memorized just like objects, connecting with other ideas or thoughts such as a sound or an image, an emotion or a memory. And how our brains process odours remains a mystery – one that is impossible to test in the same way as, say, hearing or vision.

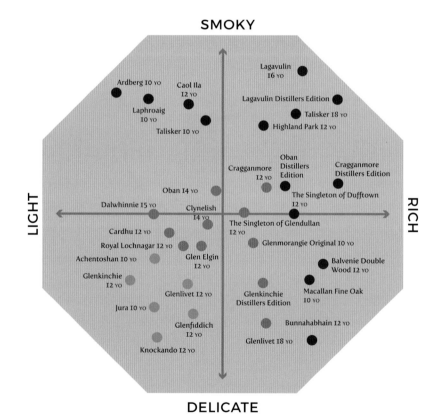

SMOKY

Lagavulin 16 YO

Ardberg 10 YO Caol Ila 12 YO

Lagavulin Distillers Edition

Laphroaig 10 YO Talisker 18 YO

Talisker 10 YO Highland Park 12 YO

Cragganmore 12 YO Oban Distillers Edition Cragganmore Distillers Edition

LIGHT Oban 14 YO **RICH**

Dalwhinnie 15 YO Clynelish 14 YO The Singleton of Dufftown 12 YO

The Singleton of Glendullan 12 YO

Cardhu 12 YO Glenmorangie Original 10 YO

Royal Lochnagar 12 YO

Achentoshan 10 YO Glen Elgin 12 YO Balvenie Double Wood 12 YO

Glenkinchie 12 YO Macallan Fine Oak 10 YO

Glenlivet 12 YO Glenkinchie Distillers Edition

Jura 10 YO

Bunnahabhain 12 YO

Glenfiddich 12 YO Glenlivet 18 YO

Knockando 12 YO

DELICATE

WHISKY CARTOGRAPHY
There are numerous flavour graphs and wheels in existence today, but the flavour map above was developed by British brand Diageo, and uses two axes to create a grid to compare flavours (from delicate to smoky) as well as intensity (from light to rich). It is a good way of finding your way through the complex jungle of whiskies.

THE FLAVOUR WHEEL

With more than 100 aromas to choose from, it can be hard to get your bearings during a whisky tasting. Luckily for us, during the 1970s whisky producers in Scotland collectively agreed to devise a set of common terms and groupings. In 1978, the Scotch Whisky Research Institute was commissioned to create a comprehensive whisky flavour wheel. Two master blenders and two industrial chemists spent just over a year to create this initial version.

© Scotch Whisky Research Institute

HOW TO USE THE WHEEL

The wheel comprises three discs, each one representing the primary, secondary or tertiary aromas. The easiest way to use it is to start with the outer disc, which indicates what you may be able to pick up in your glass, then work your way through to the centre. There are two additional versions of the wheel, which were created during the 2000s. One of these sets out ten primary aromas, and also takes into account the intensity of the whisky on a scale of one to three.

WHAT ABOUT WHISKEYS?

There is also a flavour wheel designed especially for bourbons, which is based around five principal aromas.

DIFFERENT TYPES OF WHISKY

To create Scotch, bourbon or rye involves very different production methods, which means that each spirit has a very distinct flavour. Which is the best? That's all down to personal taste!

BOURBON

AROMATIC PROFILE

Sweet
Woody with notes of vanilla

DISTINGUISHING FEATURES

Must be produced in the USA
Must contain 51% corn (maize)
Must be aged for at least 2 years
Aged in new, lightly charred American oak casks
Must not exceed 62.5% ABV before ageing

AGEING

2–8 years
Must be aged for at least
2 years in a new cask

FAMOUS BRAND

Maker's Mark

TENNESSEE

AROMATIC PROFILE

Sweet, with hints of charcoal

DISTINGUISHING FEATURES

Must be produced in Tennessee
Must contain 51% corn (maize)
Must be aged for at least 2 years
Must be filtered using the Lincoln County Process

AGEING

2–4 years
Must be aged at least
2 years and filtered
through charcoal

FAMOUS BRAND

Jack Daniel's

G | THE LINCOLN COUNTY PROCESS

As you may have guessed, this process takes its name from its geographic region of origin in Lincoln County, Tennessee, although its exact origin remains hazy. The technique involves filtering whiskey through a 3m-thick (10ft) stack of maple-wood charcoal, drop by drop, in a process lasting several days. The result is a liquor with a distinctive mellow taste, and it is this process that marks the difference between Tennessee whiskey and bourbon.

SCOTCH

AROMATIC PROFILE

More or less peaty, with fruity notes

DISTINGUISHING FEATURES

Must be distilled in a Scottish distillery
Must be aged in casks for at least 3 years
Must be bottled at a minimum of 40% ABV

AGEING

3–30 years or more
Distilled at least twice,
aged for at least 3 years in
bourbon or wine casks

FAMOUS BRAND

Johnnie Walker

RYE

AROMATIC PROFILE

Light and spicy, with a slight bitterness

DISTINGUISHING FEATURES

Must be produced in the USA
Must contain at least 51% rye. Must be aged in casks for
at least 2 years. Must not exceed 80% ABV.

AGEING

2–10 years
Must be aged for at
least 2 years in a new
or pre-filled cask

FAMOUS BRAND

Knob Creek

CANADIAN

AROMATIC PROFILE

Light or full-bodied and very versatile

DISTINGUISHING FEATURES

Must be aged at least 3 years
Must contain at least 40% ABV

AGEING

3–6 years
Must be aged for at
least 3 years in a new
or pre-filled cask

FAMOUS BRAND

Canadian Club

IRELAND

AROMATIC PROFILE

Mellow; toasted honey

DISTINGUISHING FEATURES

Must be distilled in Ireland
Must be aged for at least 3 years in wooden casks
Must be distilled to no more than 47.4% ABV

AGEING

3–12 years
Aged for at least 3 years in
bourbon or wine casks

FAMOUS BRAND

Jameson

Different types of whisky

TASTING NOTES

You know that feeling of pleasure you get when you are eating or drinking something really special? Then, a week or so later, when you remember the meal, you have real trouble recalling what it was that was so good about it all? This, in essence, is what tasting notes are for: helping to capture those moments in words. It takes a bit of effort and motivation to fill them in, but it's worth doing, as it will heighten your enjoyment and appreciation of every tasting.

FOR BEGINNERS

For a beginner, a whisky tasting is already a full-on experience that does not need to be made even more complex with reams of tasting notes. The main thing at the beginning is to note down simply what you like or dislike. For example: 'smoky aroma is too strong' or 'delicate on the palate' or 'very light in colour.' There's no need at this stage to use fancy words that won't make any sense when you read them back later; just aim to write down something understandable – something that means something to you. Don't get too influenced by what you are hearing, either. If one of your friends is picking up notes of 'peach and baked apples' but you aren't, then there's no need to note it down. You mght find that making your own appeciation scale – marks from one to ten, for example – or a system of star ratings helps.

.../.../...

Distillery/Brand/Reference:

Name:

Place of purchase:

What I like:

What I don't like:

Score: / 10

TASTING NOTES
FOR BEGINNERS

AVOID THESE ERRORS

- Writing down only the name of the distillery. It will be impossible to track the specific bottle later. Most distilleries have an average of ten different whiskies, and often more.
- Writing too fast and illegibly. You'll never be able to decipher the scribble.
- Writing your tasting notes later on. The most likely outcome is you'll get it all mixed up – or worse still, simply not write the notes at all.
- Not noting down where the whisky was purchased. Trying to buy the bottle again could prove an impossible task.
- Going too fast. Proceeding at a gentle pace will allow you to discover more, and make it easier to discern aromas and describe what you can smell.
- Not re-reading your tasting notes. If you're only writing them so they can collect dust, then you may as well save yourself the effort.

LEARN TO LOVE SURPRISES

It's worth knowing that for any given whisky, the tasting notes can vary from one day to the next. But don't panic. It's simply a question of how the taster is feeling on that day, along with the circumstances of the tasting. And let's not forget the most important thing during any tasting: just take your time to discover what the whisky in the glass in front of you has to offer.

ADVANCED LEVEL

If you're already used to whisky tastings, then it will be time to get into a little more depth, as this will allow you to discover even more about the whisky and heighten the pleasure of the whole tasting experience. The following notes might be helpful.

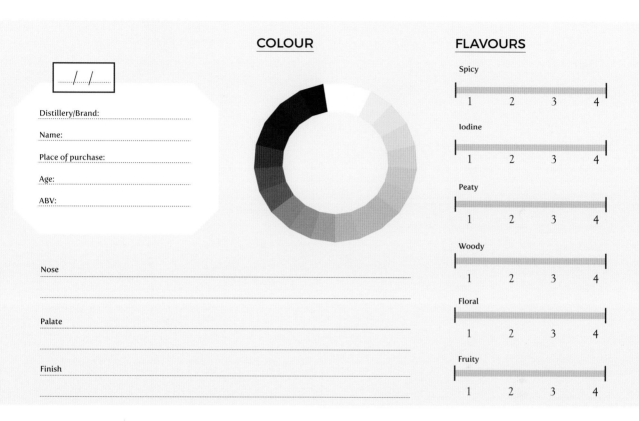

Distillery/Brand:

Name:

Place of purchase:

Age:

ABV:

Nose

Palate

Finish

COLOUR

FLAVOURS

Spicy
1   2   3   4

Iodine
1   2   3   4

Peaty
1   2   3   4

Woody
1   2   3   4

Floral
1   2   3   4

Fruity
1   2   3   4

HOW TO KEEP YOUR TASTING NOTES

It is best to keep them carefully filed. There are various ways of doing this:

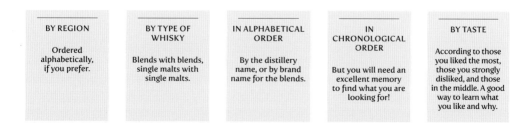

BY REGION

Ordered alphabetically, if you prefer.

BY TYPE OF WHISKY

Blends with blends, single malts with single malts.

IN ALPHABETICAL ORDER

By the distillery name, or by brand name for the blends.

IN CHRONOLOGICAL ORDER

But you will need an excellent memory to find what you are looking for!

BY TASTE

According to those you liked the most, those you strongly disliked, and those in the middle. A good way to learn what you like and why.

And above all, take the time to make (and update) a summary sheet showing all the whiskies you've tasted.

EXPERT LEVEL

This may seem a little geeky for some readers, but a tasting sheet like this gives experienced tasters almost all the information they need.

...... / ...... / ......

Distillery/brand:

Name:

Location and date of purchase:

Age:

Date of distillation:

ABV:

Price:

Other information:

Tasting glass:

COLOUR

NOSE

Intensity (first nosing):   / 10   Comments:

- mellow
- smoky
- sweet
- sherried
- acidic

CEREALS
- wine
- alcohol
- oil
- chocolate
- nuts
- fermenting wine
- mash-like
- boiled
- malt
- yeast
- flour

WINEY

FRUITY
- dried fruit
- cooked fruit
- fresh fruit
- citrus
- solvency

WOODY
- old wood
- new wood
- grilled
- spicy
- vanilla

FLORAL
- perfumed
- greenery
- plants
- lawn cuttings

SULFURY
- sulfury
- sandy
- rubbery
- drains

PEATY
- medicinal
- briny
- moss
- smoky

FEINTY
- plastic
- honey
- buttery
- leathery
- tobacco

Overall comments on the nose:

PALATE

TASTE
- salty
- sweet
- acidic
- bitter

TEXTURE
- dry
- light
- oily
- creamy
- round

PALATE
- fat
- clean
- simple
- rich
- balanced
- complex

CEREALS
- wine
- alcohol
- oil
- fermenting wine
- nuts
- chocolate
- mash-like
- boiled
- malt
- yeast
- flour

WINEY

FRUITY
- dried fruit
- cooked fruit
- fresh fruit
- citrus
- solvency

WOODY
- old wood
- new wood
- spicy
- grilled
- vanilla

FLORAL
- perfumed
- greenery
- plants
- lawn cut

SULFURY
- sulfury
- sandy
- rubbery
- drains

PEATY
- medicinal
- briny
- moss
- smoky

FEINT
- plastic
- honey
- buttery
- leathery
- tobacco

Overall comments on the palate:

FINISH

LENGTH OF FINISH

very short — short — average — long — very long

RETRO-OLFACTION
- dry
- peaty
- smoky
- winey
- syrupy
- oily

BALANCE

Balance of the nose, palate and finish:

COMMENTS ON THE FINISH:

WILLIAM PEARSON

(1761–1844)

⬦⬦⬦⬦⬦⬦⬦

The existence of Tennessee whiskey in the United States owes much to William 'Billy' Pearson.

I t all began when Pearson's mother, Tibitha Jacocks, passed on to her son the recipe for the family whiskey, based on a brew using corn (maize). The secret of its exceptional taste, however, was a filtering process through maple-wood charcoal, followed by ageing in oak casks.

The story would have ended there, had the recipe remained a family secret. But in an unexpected turn of events, Pearson had his horse stolen, and in a fit of rage he got himself a gun and set out to get his horse back from the man who had stolen it. This was a very bad idea, because Pearson lived in a pacifist Quaker community in South Carolina, where this kind of behaviour did not go down well. The result was that he and his family were kicked out.

The Pearson family moved instead to a Baptist community. Unfortunately for him, his continuing interest in distilling was frowned on by his teetotal Baptist neighbours, and they asked him to give it up. He refused, and once again found himself excluded from a church community. He decided to move to Tennessee, but his wife, Sarah, opted to stay put with the youngest four of their eight children. Pearson left for Tennessee with the four older children, and the couple eventually divorced.

Billy set up a distillery in Big Flat Creek (not far from Davy Crockett's house) close to Lynchburg, and finally sold his recipe to Alfred Eaton, who put it down in writing before, in turn, selling it on to what would become an internationally known distillery: Jack Daniel's.

AFTER THE TASTING

So you've been through the whole process, from taking an initial look at the whisky in the glass, assessing its legs, getting that first nosing, exploring the aromas, then tasting and tasting again. But just because the glasses are empty, that doesn't mean you have to call time!

SWAP YOUR IMPRESSIONS WITH YOUR FRIENDS

It's hard to emphasize enough just how much a tasting session is all about sharing and exchanging thoughts and impressions, and it's at the end of the tasting itself that the discussion and debate really start. You can also use this time to take pictures of the bottles you tasted, which can be an invaluable way of finding the one that you really liked, should you choose to buy it.

TAKE A FINAL SNIFF OF YOUR EMPTY GLASS

Here is a great reason not to launch into the washing-up too quickly: when whisky dries at the bottom of an empty glass, it releases yet more aromas, and it would be a shame to miss out on these. You could even sample them again the following morning. If you're drinking Octomore (the peatiest whisky in the world – see page 27), the aroma can linger in the empty glass for months.

HOW TO WASH TASTING GLASSES...

Some people will tell you that you should wash tasting glasses with hot water only (without any soap or detergents) to avoid soap odours clinging to the glass. The problem with this isn't one of hygiene, as the alcohol will kill the germs. Rather, over the long term there will be a build-up of oily residues on the glass. The solution is to wash the glasses by hand with a little soap, but then make sure they are well-rinsed with plenty of clean water. Dry them immediately with a clean, dry cloth. If your dishcloth is already damp, it could leave a mouldy smell on the glass.

...AND HOW TO STORE THEM

The key here is to keep the glasses upright. If they're inverted, they risk picking up an odour from the shelves of your cupboard that will taint your next tasting. Also avoid putting them into a cardboard box, as these, too, can have a characteristic smell.

STORE YOUR TASTING NOTES

The famous excuse of 'I'm too tired, I'll do it tomorrow' can be fatal, and can lead to losing, or even inadvertently binning your tasting notes in the big clear-up the next day. The best bet is to file them straight away, so you can easily find them next time.

CHECK THE LEVELS

Make sure you have enough bottled water left in stock for your next tasting session, and check the levels in each of your whisky bottles. If you have any less than one-third full, either bring them to the front so you use them up more quickly, or pour them into a smaller container so there is less air into which the alcohol can evaporate.

DRINK A BOTTLE OF WATER

After all the excitement of a whisky tasting, your palate may not relish the idea of drinking a lot of water. However, by drinking a litre of water at the end of a tasting, you'll be able to start the process of rehydration and may escape the worst of any hangover symptoms.

GET READY FOR THE NEXT TASTING

Following this tasting, discuss with your friends the kinds of whiskies they would like to discover next time. It could be helpful to use the 'flavour map' developed by Diageo (see page 80), which identifies whiskies that are either complementary or opposites in terms of flavour profile.

TAKE A TAXI HOME

Whatever people used to say about 'one for the road', whisky and driving do not mix. In any case, it's much more enjoyable to be driven home from a tasting, still enjoying the after-effects of the evening's events.

HOW TO AVOID A HANGOVER

It's the eternal question after any whisky tasting: how to avoid that inevitable hangover with its headaches, nausea, fatigue, stomachache, muscle cramps and all the other complications hangovers entail. When it comes to alcohol, the more we drink, the more dehydrated we get.

01

DURING THE EVENING:
A GLASS OF WATER BETWEEN EACH GLASS OF WHISKY

This is the best of all ways to avoid the effects of alcohol the following day (or during that same night) and is excellent for counteracting any dehydration effects.

02

A BOTTLE OF WATER BEFORE BED

Even if you've been drinking water between each glass of whisky, you still need to hydrate your body before going to bed. Remember to take water for the bedside table, too, as you're likely to wake up frequently during the night.

03

THE NEXT MORNING:
VITAMINS AND ZINC

A generous dose of fruit and vegetables the next day will do you a lot of good, replacing vitamins and working off the excesses of the previous evening. Oysters, if you like them, are rich in zinc, which will also help you feel healthy, while black radish is said to be great for a healthy liver.

GEORGE'S RECIPE

Here is a recipe for a luxurious fruit juice to make at home, rich in vitamins A and C, along with essential minerals and plenty of water. Simply peel and cut up the fruit, and put the whole lot into a blender.

1 orange
½ pineapple
½ melon (or ¼ watermelon)
1 kiwi

½ cucumber
juice of ½ lime

Serve in a large glass, with plenty of ice.

Serge Gainsbourg's hangover cure

A celebrated drinker as well as a world-renowned songwriter and musician, legend has it that Gainsbourg's go-to hangover cure was to drink a Bloody Mary – a nice healthy tomato juice with a generous slug of vodka. To make your own, mix 1 part vodka with 2 parts tomato juice, a dash of lemon juice and Tabasco sauce.

04

THROUGHOUT THE NEXT DAY

Continue rehydrating. If you get fed up with water, switch to soup, or maybe a herbal tea. Avoid coffee. Eat food that is rich in vitamins, such as bananas or oranges. And if you have a stomachache, try a teaspoon of bicarbonate of soda (baking soda) in a glass of water.

05

THE FOLLOWING EVENING
(IF YOU'RE BRAVE ENOUGH)

Time for a few more drinks with your friends. Hair of the dog, as they say. Fight fire with fire!

MEANWHILE, IN SOUTHEAST ASIA...

If you travel in Southeast Asia, there's a good chance someone will suggest that you try a drink based on turmeric. This is a plant that is often used in the west as a spice, and is said to have antioxidant and anti-inflammatory qualities. If your stomach is up to it, you could also test one of the many hangover potions sold in Japan, some based on watermelon, liquorice, or even clams.

How to avoid a hangover

WHISKY CLUBS

They may have a rather fusty image, calling to mind old men in tweed suits, but a contemporary whisky club can be an excellent place to go a little further in your whisky-tasting adventures.

HOW TO CHOOSE YOUR WHISKY CLUB

- **Is it the right level for you?** It's best not to choose a whisky club purely on the basis of picking the one closest to home. Do some background research, and see if they welcome beginners, or people at a similar level of experience to you. Many people enter a whisky club with high hopes and can end up disappointed.

- **What do they drink?** Some clubs only bring selected and unique bottles to tastings. This may or may not be what you're looking for. In some cases, clubs do their own bottling and sell them as part of the club membership.

WHISKY A GO GO: NOT THAT KIND OF WHISKY CLUB

Not a whisky-tasting club, of course, but actually a nightclub, Whisky a Go Go opened in 1964 on Sunset Strip in West Hollywood, California, and took its name from a Parisian bar of the same name that was popular with servicemen after the Second World War. The Rolling Stones song 'Going to a Go Go' was inspired by this bar, which also hosted Jim Morrison and The Doors. The venue (with a capacity of just 500) became a rock-and-roll legend, although local police hated the place and thought the name should be changed as it risked corrupting its young clientele.

WHISKY LIVE:
THE GLOBAL EXHIBITION

Whisky Live is the biggest exhibition of whisky in the world, consisting of shows taking place across the globe, where visitors can taste up to 160 different brands, from bourbons to the most esoteric and little-known whiskies out there. There are tastings, master classes, and cocktail bars, making it an unmissable event for any whisky-lover.

OUT OF TOWN

They may be hard to find, but there are usually whisky clubs in larger provincial towns and cities. If you've found a good whisky supplier, they may be the best people to ask about the existence of whisky clubs.

THE SCOTCH MALT WHISKY SOCIETY

This is the biggest club of whisky enthusiasts in the world, founded in 1983 in Edinburgh, and currently counting more than 30,000 members across the globe. Club members get to sample exceptional whiskies from almost all Scottish distilleries, with casks bought direct from some of them, selected by an expert tasting panel. Bottles have their own SMWS labelling, and are sold exclusively to members. After struggling financially, the society was sold to The Glenmorangie Company, but subsequently sold back to private investors around a decade later. Annual membership is about the same price as a decent bottle of whisky.

STAYING IN: FLAVIAR

Flaviar offers a different approach to the tasting club, delivering themed tasting boxes direct to members' homes. Members are able to add bottles to their own digital home bar so that Flaviar can make recommendations tailored to their tastes. Working directly with distillers, bars and brands, Flaviar also organizes events for members and boasts exclusive access to special collections, rare and hard-to-find spirits and private bottlings.

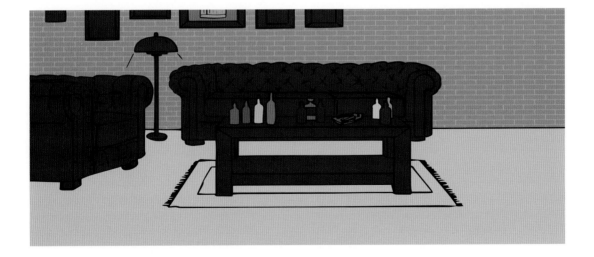

N̄ 3
BUYING WHISKY

B uying whisky can quickly become a confusing and expensive nightmare, given the apparently limitless choice of brands and options. This chapter aims to help you to get your bearings and think more strategically about buying choices, so you can build up a whisky bar your friends will envy – all without breaking the bank!

THE RIGHT BOTTLE FOR THE RIGHT OCCASION

Where and when you happen to be drinking will have a big influence on what kind of whisky you might choose. Here is a round-up of some possible scenarios.

IN THE NIGHTCLUB

First of all, forget about ordering a top-rate single malt and savouring it at your leisure. Instead, it's probably better to go for a thirst-busting whisky, something you can drink with plenty of ice, such as a Kentucky bourbon or a Scotch blend. The most important factor is price, rather than brand, as ideally you won't really get a chance to concentrate too much on what's in your glass.

THE COCKTAIL BAR

There is a common misconception that whisky cocktails should use low-quality whisky. The reality is that a bad whisky will make a bad cocktail. Think about the characteristics of the whisky; if it is excessively peaty, it will overwhelm all the other ingredients. Conversely, if the whisky is too mild, it will fail to counterbalance the rest of the drink. Scottish or Japanese blended whisky is a good cocktail base, as is Maker's Mark or American rye.

AFTER WORK

We all have our favourite bottle that we keep buying year after year. The problem is, with constant innovation from many distilleries, your favourite whisky might disappear from the range or become too pricey. There are two solutions:
- Drink a chilled bourbon on ice;
- Try a 'No Age Statement' (NAS) single malt. These are made to last, and will not meet the fate of some of their counterparts with the passage of time.

In some countries, whisky has been regarded purely as an apéritif: something to be enjoyed before a meal begins. However, it's also possible to enjoy whisky during a meal and, of course, afterwards, where it's regarded as a *digestif*. What's more, if you're a cigar smoker, the two work together particularly well.

To share with your worst enemy

There are three options here. One is a cask-strength whisky (65 per cent ABV) that you would serve, of course, without water and without warning. The insanely high alcohol level will bring a tear to the eyes, although if your worst enemy is a whisky connoisseur, they may well enjoy the experience. Another option is to offer a bottle of 'whisky' that is a blend of a rum-type molasses-based spirit plus a whisky blend (these are often made in India), which will provide an unexpected taste. Or alternatively, buy the very cheapest bottle you can find in the local supermarket.

To impress the in-laws

Again, you have several options. One is a whisky from an unexpected country, such as Tasmania or Sweden (to name but two), or a rare and fine bottle from one of their favourite brands, although that may take some time to find, whether online or at various whisky suppliers. Alternatively, if you don't get on with them very well, consider the section above.

As a holiday souvenir

Maybe you would like to rediscover that idyllic holiday retreat, and recreate those lazy apéritifs drunk while watching the sun go down? If your holiday was in France, you'll find distilleries in many regions (Brittany, Normandy, Champagne, Lorraine and so on). If you went to Scotland, finding souvenir bottles won't be a problem. And as whisky culture expands across the world, a souvenir bottle may be easier to find than you think.

The right bottle for the right occasion

HOW TO READ
A WHISKY LABEL

Don't be taken in by the slick cardboard tubes with fancy metal lids: the most important thing about the packaging of any whisky is the label on the bottle. Here's a guide to what to look for.

THE LEGAL STUFF

THE OPTIONAL STUFF

A SPECIAL CASE: AMERICAN BOURBON

With American whiskies alcoholic strength is calculated in 'proof', where one degree of proof is equivalent to 0.5 per cent ABV. This is why the alcohol numbers on a bottle of bourbon look shockingly high, but just remember: a reading of 86 degrees proof is only 43 per cent ABV.

ALCOHOL CONTENT

Expressed as a percentage by volume (% vol) or percentage of alcohol by volume (% ABV) or simply as a percentage.

QUANTITY CONTAINED IN THE BOTTLE

Expressed in litres, centilitres or millilitres: e.g., 0.75l, 75cl, 750ml.

While the legal information does not get you very far, the rest of the label contains the vital information that will help you make a choice.

THE NAME

For single malts, the label shows only the name of the distillery. For blends, the brand name is shown.

THE AGE

By law, the age must refer to the age of the youngest whisky used in that particular bottling. So your 12-year-old whisky will contain whisky that has been aged for 12 years, but also other whisky that may be somewhat older, giving it more structure and reinforcing the unique style of that particular distillery.

GEOGRAPHICAL LOCATION

If the label says 'Scotch Whisky' then this is a guarantee that it was distilled and bottled in Scotland. All Scottish single malts must also specify their region (Speyside, Highland, Lowland, Campbeltown or Islay). In a similar way, when you read 'Tennessee Whiskey' on a label, this guarantees that the whiskey has been made in Tennessee in the USA.

WHISKY Scotland 12 YEARS OLD Speyside

43% vol. 75 cl

THE RISE OF NO AGE STATEMENT

If the whisky label does not contain a specific age, this is not an oversight, but an example of the increasing prevalence of 'no-age-statement' bottles, or NAS for short. So why doesn't the bottle reveal its age? It's partly to do with the recent boom in whisky consumption, which has forced distilleries to start dipping into their younger casks to help meet demand. They could state, say, five years, on the bottle, but this would undersell a whisky of which more than 80 per cent of the contents is probably much older. So the alternative is to offer no age statement at all, and in recent years NAS bottles have become the norm – and age-statement bottles have become more expensive. Distilleries, in turn, have been forced to consider means of ageing casks on a more industrial scale to plan for future demand. And as for quality, are NAS bottles systematically inferior to the age-statement ones? Not necessarily, and many NAS bottles from Islay and Japan have been a huge success. It just doesn't work out so well in every case, however.

MORE ON THE BOTTLE LABEL

CASK STRENGTH

This means that the whisky has not been mixed with water at the bottling stage. The strength of the spirit is higher than 50 per cent ABV. Normally the number of casks that make up its composition is also shown.

SMALL BATCH

The result of blending a limited number of casks (usually around ten). This technique is widely used in the USA.

SINGLE CASK

The bottled whisky comes from a single cask, rather than a blend of casks. The distillery's specific cask number is generally added on the label, along with the bottling date.

NATURAL COLOUR

This means that no artificial colouring has been added to the whisky.

THE TYPE OF CASK USED FOR FINISHING

A reference to a 'finish' cask means that a second cask was used at the end of the ageing process to add a final touch (e.g. sherry casks or a bourbon barrel).

FIRST FILL

This is the first time a specific cask (a former sherry or bourbon cask, for example) has been used to age whisky, meaning that this whisky will have gained the strongest-possible aromas from the cask (compared with the next whisky to use this cask in the 'second fill'. Whisky from a first-fill sherry cask tends to be more expensive.

01
CASK STRENGTH

02
SMALL BATCH

03
SINGLE CASK

04
NATURAL COLOUR

05
FINISH

06
FIRST FILL

How to read a whisky label

WHERE TO BUY WHISKY

It is easy enough to find whisky in a shop, but finding good bottles at a great price is a bit more complex.

THE SUPERMARKET

The drinks section of any supermarket (or the whiskey section of a US liquor store) will have always have plenty of bottles of whisky to choose from, which can make the whole process seem even more daunting. The problem can be that most of the bottles are mediocre blends from fairly unknown brands. But sometimes, in the midst of all these, you will find a few interesting bottles at knock-down prices.

There could be some psychology at work here: finding a bargain on what could be seen as a luxury purchase could prompt other members of the shopper's household to feel entitled to pick up a bargain 'luxury' of their own: 'If you're getting that whisky, I'm getting those headphones!'

Here are some essential supermarket buys:

LAPHROAIG
10YO, peaty

ABERLOUR
12YO, sherry cask

GLENFIDDICH
1YO, Classic Speyside

SPECIAL OFFERS AND PROMOTIONS

Supermarkets sometimes put on special wine or whisky events, where you may be lucky enough to find your favourite bottles at greatly reduced prices. It's best not to expect miracles from such offers, though, so keep your eyes open and read the labels carefully! There's usually a bigger focus on marketing than on actual products, but even so, you could pick up a few bargains.

ONLINE

You can buy pretty much anything online, and whisky is no exception. There are plenty of undrinkable bottles out there, but you will also find (if you have time) some hidden gems – or indeed, the chance to discover much more about individual bottles, or bottles that are no longer in production.

Three useful sites:

THEWHISKYEXCHANGE.COM
A huge range of whisky of all types from all over the world, with intuitive search tools to help you navigate what appears to be an endless selection. There are nearly 3,000 single malts listed on the site. Ships worldwide.

UISUKI.COM/EN
If you are looking for Japanese whisky, then this is the site for you. Passionate about Japan and its whisky and packed with useful buying and tasting advice, this website will have you planning your next holiday!

LOVESCOTCH.COM
This site offers more than just Scotch – it has a range of whiskies and liquors. Most online whisky retailers are UK-based so this is a good option for US whisky fans to avoid high shipping and customs fees.

THE WHISKY SHOP

A good whisky merchant can change your approach to whisky forever. The passion and knowledge possessed by such specialists are the fundamental elements that will help to perfect your knowledge and guide you deeper and deeper into this incredible world.

How to spot a good one:

At first glance, it is hard to tell whether your whisky shop is going to be all that you're hoping for. Here are some clues.

Good whisky merchants will ask you:
• If you are choosing for yourself or as a gift;
• If the recipient likes peated whisky or not;
• What your price range is.

They should have a few opened bottles for you to taste. What better way to make up your own mind and decide if you are going to like what you buy?

They will be talking passionately about the distillery and the bottle itself. Someone who knows the product will be able to talk to you about every detail.

They will be familiar with whisky tastings and tell you about a whisky that they have particularly enjoyed, without trying to force a sale.

DOES SIZE MATTER?

Some whisky merchants are constantly expanding their whisky range, but this isn't necessarily a good thing. The idea of a 'curated' collection of high-quality products that still have a breadth across a range of tastes and intensities is better than a shelf containing dozens of bottles that are almost indistinguishable in taste.

YOUR OWN WHISKY BAR

Building up your own whisky bar will depend in part on your own taste preferences — and also, of course, on your budget. Whatever you choose, always try to taste a whisky before buying to add to your collection, either at your whisky merchant or in a bar, to avoid any unpleasant surprises when you get home.

START WITH A PLAN

First off, don't panic. This is not going to be a huge enterprise, and all you need to do is decide how to go about it. There are two main options. Either you already know what you like, and want to build your collection around a specific whisky, in which case simply take that bottle to your whisky supplier, and they will help you to do the rest. Alternatively, you may want to build a bar with samples of many different kinds of whisky (see right).

a classic Speyside

a peated whisky

whisky aged in sherry casks

a bourbon

you can add a 'rest of the world' whisky from India, Australia, and so on

AT THE SUPERMARKET

You probably won't get the expert advice here, nor the chance to taste the whisky before you buy it, but you will almost certainly find some useful bottles to add to your bar, at reasonable prices, too. Here are some suggestions:

SINGLE MALTS				BLENDS	
Laphroaig 10 YO	Glenfiddich 12 YO	Aberlour 12 YO	Talisker 10 YO (but increasingly difficult to find)	Johnnie Walker Black Label	Ballantine's 17 YO

At the whisky merchant

There is no need to break the bank to find good bottles at a specialist supplier. A 12-year-old Glendronach, a ten-year-old Benromach or a Laphroaig Quarter Cask are affordable bottles to get started with.

A whisky for my cocktails

Think about buying a bottle specifically for use in making whisky cocktails so that you don't have to pour your favourite single malt into the cocktail shaker. But don't go too downmarket; a decent blend or a bourbon will do the trick.

01
Mix your worst whisky with at least two other whiskies

02
Keep to the following proportions: 2 parts of bad whisky to 1 part of the good one (which is less risky in case you have to throw it down the sink!)

03
Only mix enough for just one tumbler of whisky, not more

04
Let your blend rest for a few hours in a closed glass container

The worst bottle in your bar

Let's be honest: we've all owned a terrible bottle of whisky at one time or another. Either through our own rash purchase, or when one of our friends (or enemies) was kind enough to give it to us. If the idea of drinking it sends chills down your spine, there is something you could try; how about creating your own blend? Be careful, though. There will be a lot of trial and error required before showing it off to your friends. Best to follow the four steps above.

A tasting kit

If you want to watch your budget and be sure of your tastes before buying, here is an ideal solution: a box of whisky samples, where each

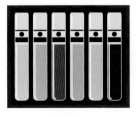

tube is equivalent to about two glasses. Several brands have specialized in this approach, which is an excellent – and relatively inexpensive – way of finding where your preferences lie.

HOW TO STORE WHISKY

As with any alcoholic drink, you'll need to follow a few basic rules to keep your stock of whisky in tip-top condition. And if you can do that, you will then get the best-possible results from your tastings.

DON'T STORE IT LIKE WINE

If you try to store a bottle of whisky as you would a bottle of wine (on its side) then you could be disappointed. As we all know, wine is stored on its side, in a cellar, to keep the corks moist and allow it to improve as it ages. Then, once opened, it is pretty much finished within 24 hours, unless you plan to use it for cooking. With whisky, it's a different story. Why? Because whisky, once bottled, is a finished product, and its corks are designed for multiple usages (see page 106). A 15-year-old whisky will remain a 15-year-old whisky, even if you keep it for a further 25 years.

THE TEMPERATURE

You don't need a cellar to keep whisky. Room temperature will be perfectly OK, whether or not the seal on your bottle has already been broken.

HOW LONG WILL IT LAST?

If your bottle is tightly stoppered and stored in the right conditions, it will keep well for a good ten years. Watch out, though, for a dodgy cork, which can appear in a whisky as it does in the world of wine. And for very strong whisky (cask strength, at more than 60 per cent ABV) the alcohol can cause the cork to dry out. The best bet is to check the state of the corks in your opened bottles fairly regularly for damage or drying, and replace them if necessary (using corks kept over from finished bottles). Nobody wants to find bits of cork floating in their glass – nor indeed to discover that the alcohol has simply evaporated!

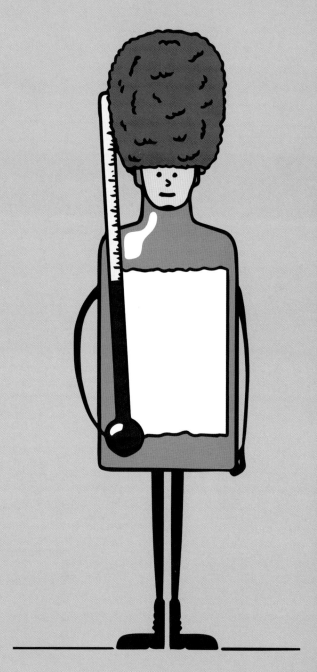

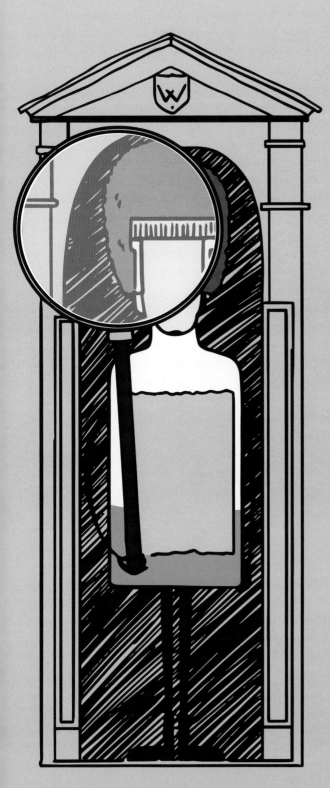

Once it's open

When air enters the bottle, it comes into contact with the surface of the whisky and causes oxidation, an effect that will be more marked as the volume of air increases in the bottle. If the bottle is less than one-third full, it's worth finishing the bottle during the coming months, or else you could consider decanting it into a smaller container with less room for air. (Remember to stick a label on the new bottle so you know what it contains, though!)

Upright or on its side?

Upright, always. Otherwise, the liquid will be in contact with the cork, which is a thing to be avoided at all costs.

Daylight or darkness?

Many whiskies today are sold in attractive presentation tubes or boxes. This is not just about marketing; it is also a question of keeping the whisky out of the light, which can affect not only its colour but also its flavours. So if your whisky is not kept in a box, best to store it in a cupboard.

ALL ABOUT THE CORK

*You might think that the humble cork is there simply to close the bottle.
That's partly true, but there's a bit more to it than that!*

WINE VS WHISKY

When it comes to storing wine, bottles are laid down
sideways so the corks are kept moist by the wine, expanding
to ensure the bottle remains sealed. Wine doesn't need air
to breathe while inside the bottle (despite what people
may tell you to the contrary). And once a bottle is opened,
the cork's work is more or less done. For whisky, however,
the cork has a lot more to do. It must be able to withstand
alcohol at 40 per cent and higher (up to 60 per cent in some
cases) ABV and then, once opened, continue to provide an
airtight seal for years to come.

CAN WHISKY BE 'CORKED'?

We all know that wine can be 'corked', but how about
whisky? It's rare, but it does happen, and occasionally a
whisky bottle can suffer from a rotten cork. You'll smell it
immediately, and it's even more obvious in the taste, which
is something like rancid nuts and damp cardboard. You may
even find mould on the cork: the result of a concentration
of nano-particles within the structure of the cork itself.
If you do find a defective cork, simply take the bottle back
to the shop and get it replaced.

WHEN THE CORK BREAKS

Opening a bottle of whisky that has been left for several
months can be a delicate operation. If you twist it too
harshly, or are simply unlucky, there's a chance the cork
will break off. However, this does not need to be a complete
crisis, and an 'emergency whisky survival kit' will get you
back on track. You need:
- An empty whisky bottle that has been washed and rinsed,
  complete with a serviceable cork;
- A small strainer to pick up any pieces of broken cork
  when you pour the whisky from its original bottle into
  the new one;
- A bottle opener to pull out the remaining part of the cork
  from the bottle neck.

Aim to keep the bottle upright (rather than on the diagonal)
and pull out the cork smoothly with the corkscrew, expecting
it to fragment further as it emerges.

THE ONLY WAY IS UP

Keeping bottles stocked horizontally may seem like a good idea, on the basis that the cork is less likely to dry out. However, it is actually the worst possible idea and could ruin your whisky, because the alcohol's strength will damage the cork, which in turn will taint your whisky.

UPSIDE-DOWN THINKING

Some experts recommend that you turn a bottle upside down from time to time, again with the idea of preventing the cork from drying out. However, not everyone agrees with this idea, given the continuing risk of the cork being attacked by alcohol and becoming more fragile.

soaked cork   dry cork

THE WAX-SEALED CORK

At some point, you'll find yourself face to face with a wax-sealed stopper (especially if you want to drink Maker's Mark). It is a joy to look at, and steeped in history, but a real pain to open if you don't have the knack. Here's how to do it:
1. Pierce the wax with your corkscrew.
2. Pull up the cork halfway.
3. Cut off the wax with a knife (this is essential, or wax will end up in the whiskey).
4. Pull the cork out completely. Don't chuck it in the bin, as you will need to use it as the stopper in the future.

THE OTHER CORK

All this talk about cork brings to mind County Cork in Ireland, which is home to the biggest distillery in the republic: Midleton Distillery, producing more than 19 million litres of alcohol each year, which means a lot of corks. Among its most famous brands you will find Jameson, Paddy and Tullamore Dew.

All about the cork

THE MARKETING MACHINE

The whisky business is all about expertise. But there is also an element of smoke and mirrors involved!

WATCH OUT FOR ROMANCE

In some countries of the world (such as France) there are laws designed to restrict the advertising of alcohol, controlling the images or messages that can be used. This has led to some distilleries getting more creative, building their brand around a 'story' about their history or traditions, rather than through images of the drinks themselves. Remember, though: you're buying a whisky, not a beautiful story!

OVER-THE-TOP LABELS

Some brands don't hold back when it comes to trumpeting the qualities of their whisky on the label, using words like 'exceptional', 'rare', 'premium', 'pure' and so on. In reality, there's a big chance of reading all that and still being disappointed.

CELEBRITY ENDORSEMENTS

It can be tempting to think that if a whisky is good enough for a Hollywood A-lister or for one of the most famous ex-footballers in the world, then it must be a pretty good whisky, and certainly good enough for me. Just remember: distilleries have plenty of marketing tricks up their sleeves, and celebrity endorsements is a key one. It doesn't mean, however, that you will actually *like* that particular whisky!

BOXES AND TUBES

One of the most-used marketing tools is the box or tube that contains the whisky bottle itself. The box is actually there to protect the whisky from light, although each year whisky brands come up with more and more elaborate ideas for the packaging, whether for Father's Day, the holiday season, or simply to mark a brand's anniversary. Again, think about the label rather than the box – unless you're a collector of whisky boxes, of course.

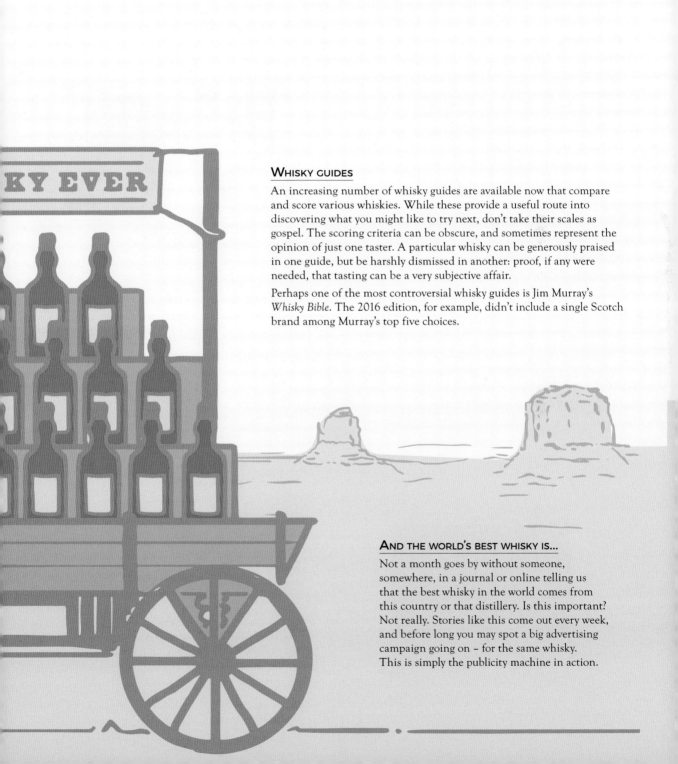

Whisky guides

An increasing number of whisky guides are available now that compare and score various whiskies. While these provide a useful route into discovering what you might like to try next, don't take their scales as gospel. The scoring criteria can be obscure, and sometimes represent the opinion of just one taster. A particular whisky can be generously praised in one guide, but be harshly dismissed in another: proof, if any were needed, that tasting can be a very subjective affair.

Perhaps one of the most controversial whisky guides is Jim Murray's *Whisky Bible*. The 2016 edition, for example, didn't include a single Scotch brand among Murray's top five choices.

And the world's best whisky is...

Not a month goes by without someone, somewhere, in a journal or online telling us that the best whisky in the world comes from this country or that distillery. Is this important? Not really. Stories like this come out every week, and before long you may spot a big advertising campaign going on – for the same whisky. This is simply the publicity machine in action.

THE PRICE

◇◇◇◇◇◇◇◇◇◇◇◇◇◇◇

Behind that little white sticker is a lot more than a simple price.

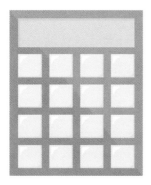

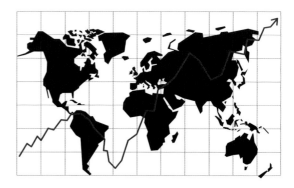

WHAT MAKES UP THE PRICE?

Your bottle of whisky contains a fair bit of tax. Beyond whatever sales tax you pay in your country (such as VAT in Europe), there will also be an excise duty: a liquor tax that dates back to the 17th century in England. This tax isn't attached to the value of a product, but to its quantity. For spirits, the higher the level of alcohol, the higher the excise duty.

INVESTING IN WHISKY

Like so many good things, whisky tends to become more valuable with age. The aim, for whisky investors, is to target only bottles with a current or potential rarity value. With skill and experience, this strategy can pay off. A bottle of whisky bought at £250 ($310) a decade ago could be worth up to £7,000 ($8,700) today. With an annual appreciation of ten to fifteen per cent, prices are currently on an upswing. One category particularly popular with investors is special-edition whisky, such as the one created by The Macallan to mark the UK's royal wedding of Kate and William; it was sold immediately after the wedding for 20 times the purchase price. Beyond all this insanity, there are also genuine collectors who simply want to build a collection of whiskies for the pure pleasure of it, and for that of future generations. Fortunately!

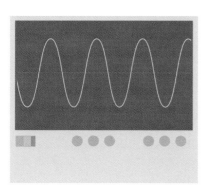

THE PRICE BAROMETER

It would be nice to have a reliable measure of the value of any particular whisky at any given time (as you might have, more or less, for a used car), but unfortunately there is no such thing. The best way to find out about the price of a specific bottle is to go online and engage with various forums, but remember: most buyers out there will be hoping to make a quick buck from your sale, so be sure to check with several sources.

If your grandparents are into their whisky (or any other spirits) it could be worth (with their permission) checking out their cupboards for any forgotten bottles that have been gathering dust over the decades. They could be worth a small fortune, and provide a rare treat at your next tasting.

How to sell your bottles

There are plenty of options, including specialist online auction sites, whisky forums, or Facebook groups dedicated to whisky. One of the most well-known sites for selling whisky is whiskyauction.com, which charges commission on each sale along with a delivery fee.

What makes a whisky unique (and expensive)?

The equation is simple enough. Thankfully, quality is generally the most important factor. Then there is the rarity value: the fewer bottles in existence, the more the value can climb. You don't need look just at older whisky, either. Some ten-year-old whiskies that have gone out of production can still hit astronomical values.

The rising cost of quality

Around ten years ago, you might still have been able to find a good whisky for around £25 ($31), but today this is becoming much more difficult. Part of the reason is down to the general increase in whisky consumption, which has seen prices rise accordingly. The other aspect is that, in the 1980s and 1990s, many distilleries were struggling, and some went bust, with the result that whisky prices fell as stocks were sold off cheap. These days, the price of a good bottle is somewhere between £35 ($43) and £60 ($74).

N⁻4
AT THE TABLE

Whisky will soon become your best friend at the dinner table. As with wine, you must be wary of bad flavour combinations that will ruin the meal, but here you can find all the information you need. With a little practise, you'll soon become a pro at whisky pairings and impress guests at every dinner!

A WHISKY DINNER

Everyone is used to the idea of serving wine with a meal, but whisky rarely springs to mind. And yet, with its an amazing range of aromas and tastes, whisky can complement an enormous variety of different foods. All of which makes it perfectly possible to serve it throughout a meal!

FOOD + WHISKY: HOW DOES IT WORK?

Alcoholic spirits (and we are talking here about drinks with more than 40 per cent ABV) have a much more complex and changing array of aromas than wines. If you serve whisky with ingredients containing water, then both the level of alcohol and its aromas can change. With so many variables, the ways of pairing whisky and food are almost endless.

01

As complements:
Food boosts the whisky's flavour and vice versa.

02

As opposites:
Strong-tasting food versus a smoky, smooth whisky.

03

Matching:
Look for flavours in the whisky to match those in the food.

JAPANESE-STYLE

Don't like the idea of neat whisky with your meal? Then take a tip from the Japanese and add plenty of water to lower its alcohol content (see page 126 on the Mizuwari).

WHAT COMES FIRST?

Should you start with the whisky or with some food? The rule of thumb is to eat first. This works especially well with foods containing fats, such as cheese, which have an appreciable effect on the whisky, making it seem less aggressive to the taste: ideal for those who typically find whisky too strong.

Avoid these traps

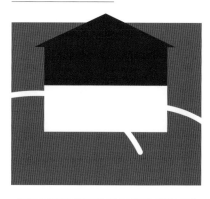

TOO MUCH SUGAR
Too much sugar in food can ruin your enjoyment
of a whisky, amplifying the presence and power
of the alcohol.

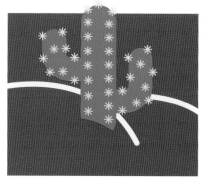

TOO MUCH SALT
A salty dish will produce an astringent reaction,
causing your mouth's mucous membranes to
contract and creating a dry or even soapy
sensation that can be deeply unpleasant.

TOO MUCH GOAT CHEESE
However much you may like goat cheese, whisky
can actually release a truly goat-like odour from it.
Depending on how much you really like goats, this
could be a little off-putting for your meal.

Diageo's Classic Malt and Food

Getting people used to the idea of drinking whisky with meals has become
a major focus for whisky brands. With this aim in mind, drinks group Diageo
produced its Classic Malt and Food initiative, coming up with food pairings
based around 13 brands within its 'classic malt' collection. Here are few
examples to tempt you:

CAOL ILA
with Camembert and tapenade

CARDHU
with Parma ham and dates

KNOCKANDO
with foie gras

TALISKER
with smoked salmon and
fromage frais

**THE SINGLETON OF
DUFFTOWN**
with praline chocolate
cookies and marmalade

The Aberlour Hunting Club

Eating in a prestigious setting with
a menu specially designed to showcase
Aberlour whiskies is what the Aberlour
Hunting Club is all about. For the
past few years, Aberlour has invited
famous chefs to propose a high-end
gastronomic menu around some of its
whiskies. Tickets are rare and highly
prized, with only a few tables available
for a limited period.

ON PAST HUNTING CLUB MENUS:

▶ *Bourgogne snails in a liquorice
broth + Aberlour 2003 White Oak*

▶ *Salmon, caviar and mustard with
soup of Duke potatoes + Aberlour
16YO Double Cask Matured*

▶ *Roasted venison tenderloin with
a grand veneur sauce + Aberlour
18YO Double Cask Matured*

▶ *Hazelnut streusel with caramelized
pears, Manjari chocolate creams,
pear and ginger sorbet + Aberlour
A'bunadh*

WHAT TO EAT WITH WHISKY

Finding yourself short of ideas when it comes to what dishes to serve with your whiskies? Don't panic. There are plenty of winning combinations that will make the most of both your cooking and your whisky collection.

GETTING STARTED

While there are no specific foods that pair well with every kind of whisky, some are easier to combine than others. So it is best to try these out first:

- Cheese: Roquefort, Camembert, mature Cheddar, Gouda or Comté.
- Chocolate: while some whiskies pair well with milk chocolate, dark chocolate tends to work best. The more cocoa content, the better.

- Cold meats and olives: these are ideal for apéritifs, and can show your friends the pleasures of mixing food with whisky.
- Fruits: an apple or pear tart is perfect. Avoid citrus fruits, as they tend to mask the taste of whisky.

WHAT DISH FOR WHICH WHISKY?

Suppose you've an opened bottle in your bar at home, and would like to try it with food. Here are some foods that pair up nicely with four distinct styles.

BRING ON THE CHEESE BOARD

Organize a tasting party with a wide selection of cheeses designed to go with a selection of whiskies. Start tasting the lightest cheese with the mildest whisky, and go up in strength with both whiskies and cheese. Some pairings will seem very ordinary, while others may be exceptional. You will get a feel for how both cheese and whisky can reinforce each other's taste.

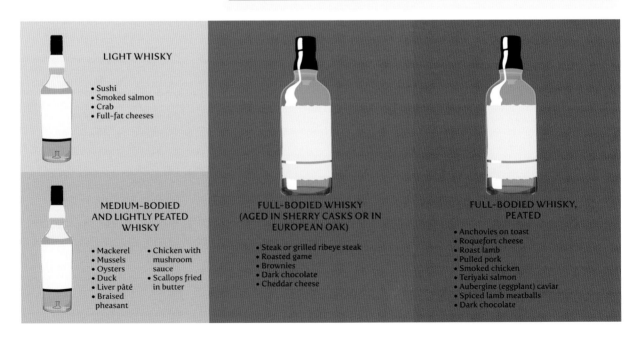

LIGHT WHISKY

- Sushi
- Smoked salmon
- Crab
- Full-fat cheeses

MEDIUM-BODIED AND LIGHTLY PEATED WHISKY

- Mackerel
- Mussels
- Oysters
- Duck
- Liver pâté
- Braised pheasant
- Chicken with mushroom sauce
- Scallops fried in butter

FULL-BODIED WHISKY (AGED IN SHERRY CASKS OR IN EUROPEAN OAK)

- Steak or grilled ribeye steak
- Roasted game
- Brownies
- Dark chocolate
- Cheddar cheese

FULL-BODIED WHISKY, PEATED

- Anchovies on toast
- Roquefort cheese
- Roast lamb
- Pulled pork
- Smoked chicken
- Teriyaki salmon
- Aubergine (eggplant) caviar
- Spiced lamb meatballs
- Dark chocolate

REGIONS AND STYLES: DOES IT WORK LIKE WINE?

When it comes to wine pairings, it seems fairly straightforward: a red Burgundy works with cheese, a Muscadet with fish, a Rioja with lamb and so forth. But what about whisky? It's much more complex, because in a specific region two neighbouring distilleries can produce completely different kinds of whiskies. The table below may prove helpful.

	MEAT, FISH, EGG	VEGETABLES	FRUIT	NUTS	CHOCOLATE	CHEESE
B BOURBON	BBQ Chicken Duck Pork	Broccoli Brussels sprouts Potatoes Roasted carrots	Apples Apricots Peaches Pears	Pecans Almonds	White chocolate	Manchego Blue cheese
R RYE	Beef Chicken Egg Mutton Salmon	Kale Brussels sprouts Potatoes Sun-dried tomatoes	Apples Pears Strawberries	Peanuts Pecans	Dark chocolate	Ricotta Cheddar
W IRISH WHISKEY	Beef Veal Game	Beans Garlic Onions Potatoes	Apples Pears	Macadamia nuts Brazil nuts	Dark chocolate	Brie Pecorino Havarti
H YOUNG HIGHLAND	Cold meat Egg Smoked salmon Tuna	Carrots Celery Lentils Wild mushrooms	Apples Dates Figs	Almonds Pistachios	Milk chocolate	Mature Gouda Cheddar Mascarpone
H HIGHLAND 15YO AND OLDER	Roast beef Lamb Turkey	Asparagus Celery Sweet potatoes	Cherries Dates Pears	Pecans Pistachios	Dark or milk chocolate	Mature Cheddar Blue cheese
L LOWLAND	Chicken Pork Steak	Chanterelle mushrooms Cucumber Courgettes (zucchini) Mushrooms Potatoes	Apricots Figs Blackberries	Macadamia nuts Almonds	Milk chocolate	Brie Young Gouda
	Egg Oysters Pigeon Salmon	Aubergine (eggplant) Red cabbage Sweetcorn (corn) Onions Potatoes Squash	Pineapple	Almonds Walnuts	Milk chocolate	Mozzarella

What to eat with whisky?

WHISKY SPECIALITIES

In both Scotland and Ireland the custom of pairing whisky with certain traditional meals goes back many generations. To this day, there are certain iconic regional dishes that, coupled with the right whisky, will prove to be a revelation on your palate!

IRISH SMOKED SALMON

The Republic of Ireland is one of the world's biggest producers of salmon. Traditionally, Irish smoked salmon is served in pubs, as well as being a classic dish on any special occasion.

WHAT TO DRINK WITH SMOKED SALMON

The smokiness of smoked salmon might prompt you to choose a peated whisky, but don't go overboard; the overall smokiness of both could ruin your appreciation of each one. Instead, opt for a whisky that is lightly peated, or one with herbal notes or iodine or spices. Good ones to try: Dalwhinnie 15YO or Talisker Storm.

INGREDIENTS
fine slices of Irish smoked salmon
2 lemons
lightly salted butter
fresh bread
coleslaw
salt and pepper

PREPARATION
Season the salmon with salt and pepper and arrange on a platter. Cut the lemons into wedges and add to the platter. Place the butter on the table. Tell your guests to help themselves!

THE FAMOUS HAGGIS

The haggis, a traditional Scottish dish, is essentially a stuffed sheep's stomach. The precise history of how this dish came into being remains a little vague. One legend has it that when Highland sheep farmers took their flocks on the long journey down to Edinburgh to sell them, they took the haggis with them to eat on the way. Traditionally, the haggis is eaten on 25 January, known as Burns Night, to celebrate the anniversary of the birth of Scottish poet, Robert Burns.

INGREDIENTS

1 sheep's stomach
1kg (2lb 4oz) sheep's offal (liver, heart)
250g (8oz) sheep's kidneys
100g (3½oz) lamb (or beef) suet
3 onions
500g (1 2ozlb) oatmeal
salt and pepper

WHAT TO DRINK WITH HAGGIS

It is best to avoid intensely peated whisky with haggis. Instead, consider one of these:
• Talisker 10YO (or if not available, Talisker Skye)
• Highland Park 12YO
• Laphroaig 10YO
• Glenlivet 18YO

If you add whisky to your haggis before cooking, it will become a 'royal haggis'.

PREPARATION

01 Thoroughly wash the sheep's stomach, turn it inside out and carefully scour the interior. Leave it to soak overnight in cold salted water.

02 Wash the offal, kidneys and suet, immerse in boiling water, add salt and allow to simmer gently for 2 hours. Drain, remove any bone, gristle or tubes, and cut up thoroughly to get a coarse, granular texture.

03 Peel the onions and blanch them in boiling water. Remove and chop finely, reserving the boiling liquid.

04 Gently toast the oats until they are lightly browned.

05 Mix together all the ingredients, adding the onion water, and gently knead into a flexible ball.

06 Spoon the stuffing into the sheep's stomach to around two-thirds of its capacity. Remove any air bubbles and sew up the stomach. Secure with string around the outside.

07 Prick the skin with the point of a knife to prevent the haggis from exploding during cooking, and then immerse it in a large pan of boiling water. Reduce the heat, cover, and let it simmer for 3–4 hours. Remove from the pan and keep it warm, removing the string.

08 To serve, open up the stomach and remove the stuffing, spooning it onto each plate. Serve with mashed potatoes, leeks, fresh bread and butter.

COOKING WITH WHISKY

Another great way to enjoy whisky is to use it in cooking. There's no advantage in using your most expensive bottle, though!

WHISKY SAUCE

INGREDIENTS
3 shallots, finely chopped
2 tbsp vegetable oil
100ml (3½fl oz) whisky
3 tsp meat stock (veal, beef)
2 tsp sugar
100ml (3½fl oz) water

PREPARATION
Heat the oil in a heavy-based pan over a medium heat. Add the shallots and sauté until tender. Add the whisky and stock, sugar and water and let it bubble until the sauce has reduced. Serve with a joint of beef.

WHISKY MARMALADE

INGREDIENTS
1.3kg (3lb) Seville oranges (organic if possible)

1kg (2lb 4oz) sugar
100ml (3½fl oz) whisky

PREPARATION

 01 Scrub the oranges and place the whole fruits into a pressure cooker. Cover with water. Bring to the boil and cook under pressure for 40 minutes. Remove from the heat and let the oranges cool in their cooking juices.

02 The next day, remove the oranges, reserving the liquid. Cut the oranges in half and scoop out the flesh, pith and pips.

03 Chop the peel into 3-cm (1-in) strips, then return them to the cooking liquid, adding the sugar and two-thirds of the whisky. Press the orange pulp through a muslin bag to extract the thick juice, which is rich in pectin, then add this to the mix.

04 Bring the marmalade mix to the boil (to 104°C/219°F). Add the rest of the whisky and mix well.

05 Transfer immediately into sterilized jars. It will be ready to enjoy as soon as it has cooled.

Yves-Marie Le Boudonnec, a well-known French butcher, adds whisky to meat as part of a two-stage maturation process. First, the meat is allowed to rest for around 20 days, during which time various enzymes tenderize the fibres. In the second stage, Le Boudonnec wraps the meat in a cloth soaked in whisky, renewing the process every ten days. The fat in the meat absorbs the whisky, adding to its exceptional taste.

IT'S FLAMING DELICIOUS!

How about a fricassée of tiger prawns (jumbo shrimps) flavoured with whisky? In your standard recipe, just add 100ml (3½fl oz) whisky and light a match. It is sure to impress!

CRANACHAN: A TRADITIONAL SCOTTISH DESSERT

INGREDIENTS

2 tbsp porridge oats
300g (10½oz) raspberries
caster sugar
350ml (12fl oz) double
   (heavy) cream
2 tbsp honey
3 tbsp whisky

PREPARATION

01 Toast the oats in a frying pan (skillet) until they start to smell nutty. Set to one side and cool.

02 Make a purée with half of the raspberries, and push through a sieve. Add sugar. Whip the double cream to soft peak stage, and add the honey and whisky to taste.

03 Add the oatmeal and whip until the mix becomes fairly firm.

04 Put a heaped tablespoon of cream in each dessert glass, then a couple of tablespoons of the oatmeal mix, then add a few whole raspberries and repeat, finishing with the cream. Chill in the fridge until needed.

N⁻5 BARS & COCKTAILS

W hether you're in front of or behind the bar, there's no other spirit out there quite like whisky. The same can be said for whisky cocktails, which have the power to transport us to another era, or even to other continents. Read on!

WHAT TO DRINK IN A BAR

*Imagine you're in a bar with some friends, family, colleagues, clients or whomever.
What are you going to order?*

CHECK OUT THE BACK OF THE BAR

If you're unfamiliar with the bar, take
a look over the bartender's shoulder
at the array of bottles on the shelves.

Be ready to walk out if:

- There is only one bottle
  of whisky;
- The only whiskies on offer
  are of the budget-priced
  supermarket variety;
- Bottles are open and covered
  in dust.

WHISKY BARS ONLY?

Of course, a whisky bar can give you
the best possible whisky-drinking
experience, with the biggest and widest
choice. But don't feel it is the only
option. Many contemporary bars and
cocktail bars also have a great bourbon
or whisky selection.

THE BEST WHISKY BAR IN THE WORLD

Take a trip to Ireland and make your way to Dingle in County
Kerry. Dick Mack's is a family-owned business on Greene Street
that has been running since 1899, with an impressive selection of
Irish whiskey and a good range from various regions of Scotland,
too. However, it's the occasional celebrity client (Sean Connery,
Julia Roberts) who has helped put Dick Mack's on the map, and
their visits are immortalized in the floor tiles, Hollywood-style.

IN THE MOOD FOR A WHISKY?

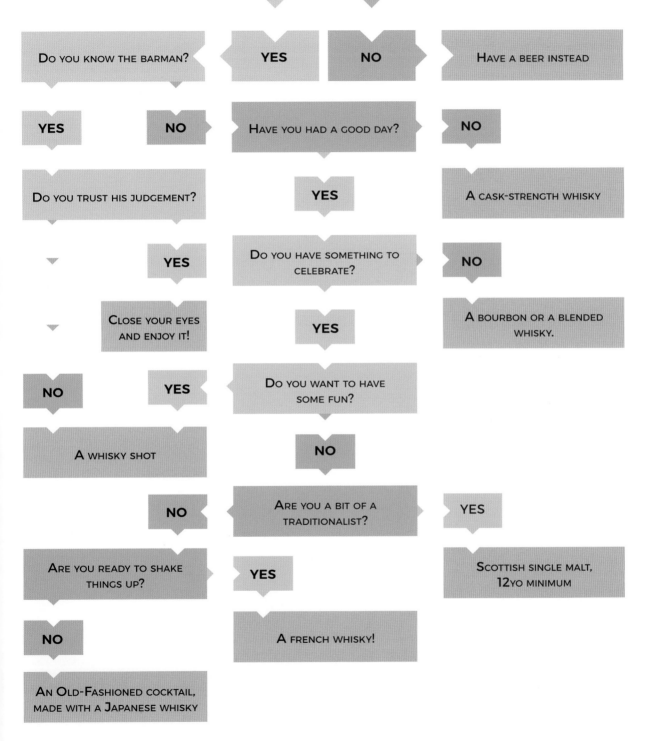

DO YOU KNOW THE BARMAN? → **YES** / **NO** → **HAVE A BEER INSTEAD**

YES / **NO**

HAVE YOU HAD A GOOD DAY? → **NO**

DO YOU TRUST HIS JUDGEMENT?

YES

A CASK-STRENGTH WHISKY

YES

DO YOU HAVE SOMETHING TO CELEBRATE? → **NO**

CLOSE YOUR EYES AND ENJOY IT!

YES

A BOURBON OR A BLENDED WHISKY.

NO / **YES**

DO YOU WANT TO HAVE SOME FUN?

A WHISKY SHOT

NO

NO

ARE YOU A BIT OF A TRADITIONALIST? → **YES**

ARE YOU READY TO SHAKE THINGS UP?

YES

SCOTTISH SINGLE MALT, 12YO MINIMUM

NO

A FRENCH WHISKY!

AN OLD-FASHIONED COCKTAIL, MADE WITH A JAPANESE WHISKY

THE MIZUWARI

'OH MY GOD!' This is the typical response of any Scotch whisky fan when first presented with a mizuwari. How can anyone really want to drown their whisky in mineral water and think this is a good idea? But there's a precise art to this practice – and if it makes the Scots grimace, it's hugely popular in Japan.

WHAT IT IS AND HOW TO SAY IT

A mizuwari is a Japanese mixture of whisky with double its volume of mineral water, and some ice cubes thrown in. The literal translation of the word means 'mixed with water'. Pronunciation is more or less how it looks when written out, although the final 'r' sounds like an 'l': *mi-zu-wah-li*.

The quantity of ice in the glass is key. The mizuwari is meant to last the duration of an entire meal. If there's insufficient ice, the drink will be too warm by the time you get to dessert; too much ice, and you'll finish your drink too soon. It may look simple, but there is an art to this.

THE RITUAL

While you may think mixing one is just a case of adding a few glugs of water to a splash of whisky, you'd be wrong. It is all in the preparation. Watching a Japanese-trained barman preparing a mizuwari presents quite a performance, with specific techniques required at each stage.

01

The tumbler is chosen with care, with a specific thickness and quality of glass.

04

The whisky is poured carefully, and delicately mixed with the ice.

02

The glass is cooled with ice cubes, which are then discarded.

05

Water is added bit by bit, with whisky aromas released at each stage.

03

Fresh ice cubes have their corners carefully rounded off, and are then placed in the glass.

06

Finally, with all the water added, the drink is mixed vigorously, but silently.

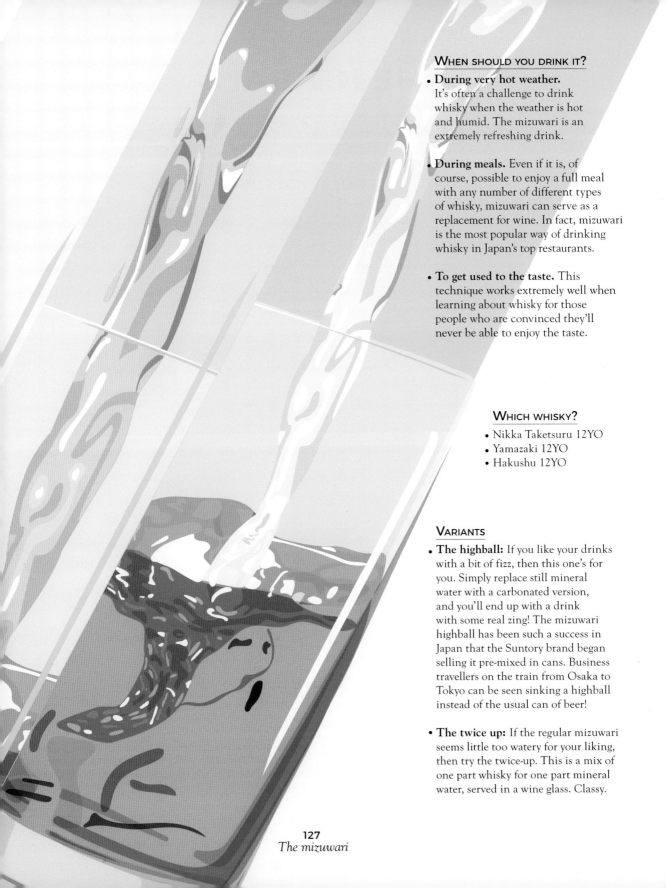

WHEN SHOULD YOU DRINK IT?

- **During very hot weather.** It's often a challenge to drink whisky when the weather is hot and humid. The mizuwari is an extremely refreshing drink.

- **During meals.** Even if it is, of course, possible to enjoy a full meal with any number of different types of whisky, mizuwari can serve as a replacement for wine. In fact, mizuwari is the most popular way of drinking whisky in Japan's top restaurants.

- **To get used to the taste.** This technique works extremely well when learning about whisky for those people who are convinced they'll never be able to enjoy the taste.

WHICH WHISKY?

- Nikka Taketsuru 12YO
- Yamazaki 12YO
- Hakushu 12YO

VARIANTS

- **The highball:** If you like your drinks with a bit of fizz, then this one's for you. Simply replace still mineral water with a carbonated version, and you'll end up with a drink with some real zing! The mizuwari highball has been such a success in Japan that the Suntory brand began selling it pre-mixed in cans. Business travellers on the train from Osaka to Tokyo can be seen sinking a highball instead of the usual can of beer!

- **The twice up:** If the regular mizuwari seems little too watery for your liking, then try the twice-up. This is a mix of one part whisky for one part mineral water, served in a wine glass. Classy.

THE ICE BALL

Invented in Japan, the ice ball could completely change how you enjoy your whisky.

A JAPANESE ART FORM

BUT WHAT IS IT?

As we all know, if you're serious about whisky, you don't chuck a load of ice cubes into your glass. But the ice ball is something else entirely. It is a beautiful, spherical, almost perfectly transparent ball of ice that will cool your whisky without diluting it, and it is yet another testament to Japanese craft skills and tradition. Carving one is a skill in itself. Many bartenders try, but only a few succeed.

THE TOOLS

Some people carve an ice ball with an extremely sharp, strong knife, although it is more common to see it done using two sharply pointed picks: a single pointed one to break down the block into cubes, and a three-pronged one for precision sculpting of the perfect spherical balls.

HOW IT'S DONE

The ideal ice ball will be perfectly spherical, carved from a block of ice, and with dimensions designed to fit your glass with millimetre precision. This helps it to cool the whisky more effectively than traditional ice cubes. The fact that it contains hardly any air bubbles not only gives it amazing transparency, but also means it will melt much more slowly in the glass.

THE ICE BALL RITUAL

01

SCULPTING THE SPHERE

Using the special ice picks, the bartender will transform a large cube of ice into a regular sphere. This demands extreme care, months of experience, and a very good eye.

CAN I TRY THIS AT HOME?

It's not advisable, given the serious risk that you could end up at the local hospital with an ice pick stuck in your hand. However, the principle of the ice ball is something you can bring to your own home whisky bar, thanks to silicone moulds designed for this very purpose. Fill them with your best mineral water (not tap water) and let them freeze. Then peel off the mould, and you're ready to enjoy the rest of the ice-ball ritual.

02

PUTTING IT INTO THE GLASS

The ice ball is slid into the empty glass and a little water is added. The bartender turns the ball rapidly several times to chill the water.

03

POURING THE WHISKY

Any water is drained from the glass. The bartender will then pour the whisky slowly and delicately over the sphere, starting at the top. The ball is moved around progressively to ensure that the temperature of the whisky is uniform throughout the glass.

IT'S ALL IN THE TIMING

An expert barman can make an ice ball in around two minutes. At typical room temperature, the ice ball will hardly melt at all during the subsequent 30 minutes, which happens to be the ideal time to spend enjoying your whisky. Contrast that with regular ice cubes, which will be reduced to a watery mess after half an hour, serving only to dilute, rather than to chill your whisky.

WHICH WHISKY FOR AN ICE BALL?

While you may imagine ice balls are designed for Japanese whiskies (and you'd be correct) they do work extremely well with many other whiskies. Which gives you yet another good reason to open a bottle and try it out!

COCKTAILS :
THE BASIC TOOLS

*You don't need to be a professional barman to make professional-looking cocktails.
But you do need a few basic tools and techniques if you're going to impress your friends
and make drinks worth drinking!*

 GEORGES' TIP

When using a mixing glass and a bar spoon, it works best to hold
the spoon gently between your thumb, index and middle fingers.

COCKTAIL SHAKER

It may be the most obvious of cocktail tools, but it's also
the most practical. As well as mixing cocktails, adding ice
to a cocktail shaker allows you to lower the temperature of
your cocktail rapidly. There are two main types of shaker,
which break down into either two or three pieces (the latter
of which contains a filter). Here's how to use one: add the
ingredients, then the ice, close the top firmly and shake
until you see a light frost appear on the surface of the shaker.
If you have trouble opening it, press hard with a diagonal
movement from bottom to top, pushing up with your thumb
– or tap the side of the shaker sharply to loosen it.

THE MIXING GLASS

Many people think that all cocktails are made in shakers,
but this isn't actually the case. Some are created in a mixing
glass, stirred rather than shaken, which is the simplest way
to make any cocktail. You need a mixing glass (the glass part
of a Boston shaker is perfectly suitable) as well as a bar spoon
– which looks like a teaspoon but with a very long handle to
reach down into the longest of drinks.

Always put your glasses in the fridge (or even in the freezer) so that they are ready for use and will keep the drink cold once it has been served.

The cocktail shaker has not really evolved much since its invention, although the current trend for internet-connected objects has also managed to reach the humble shaker. Today it is possible to connect your shaker to Bluetooth, and to use an app on your phone to help you to make cocktails. You choose the cocktail you want to make on the app, which lists the ingredients. Lights on the shaker will help you get the quantities correct, and an accelerometer in the shaker will show you how to move it correctly to create the best-possible cocktail.

THE RIGHT GLASS

In the world of cocktails, the right glass matters. You could make the best cocktail in the world, but serve it in the wrong glass and it won't shine as well as it could. So take a moment to find the glass that corresponds with your cocktail (elegant, casual, whatever) and serve it up in style.

THE JIGGER

The dose in a cocktail is crucial; getting it wrong can unbalance a drink. Classic measuring cups, known as jiggers, have a small cup (20ml/¾fl oz) and a large cup (40ml 1¼fl oz). If you don't have one but need to make a quick estimate, then a screwcap from a spirits bottle contains approximately 20ml.

THE MUDDLER

This is an essential tool to help release the aromas of fruits or spices. The trick is to press down into the mixing glass at the same time as making a circular movement with the muddler. Don't press too hard, though, and check that the mixing glass is sufficiently robust; otherwise there is a risk that the glass will shatter, which could really put a damper on the rest of your evening.

THE JULEP STRAINER

You are making a cocktail, not a stew, so remember to strain the contents of your shaker or mixing glass so that you keep only the most important part: the liquid. You can then dispose of fragments of ice or fruit that would get in the way of a great cocktail.

Cocktails: the basic tools

WHISKY-BASED COCKTAILS: THE CLASSICS

Whisky-based cocktails have been around since the 19th century, when they were the height of trendiness – and the drink of choice at all the best bars.

IRISH COFFEE

Let's not forget that some cocktails are best served warm. Irish coffee is probably one of the most well-known of all whisky-based drinks. Paradoxically, it is better known outside of Ireland than in Ireland itself, where it's mostly served to tourists. Its origins are murky, but here's one account of how it all started.

THE STORY

At the beginning of the 1940s, most transatlantic flights made a stopover at Shannon, a city in County Clare on the western side of Ireland. The story goes that a bartender came up with the idea of adding whisky to the coffee he served to American travellers, who were freezing cold in the hostile Irish climate. A traveller asked if the coffee came from Brazil, to which the bartender replied: 'No, it's Irish coffee!' There's even a plaque at Shannon Airport to commemorate the event.

INGREDIENTS

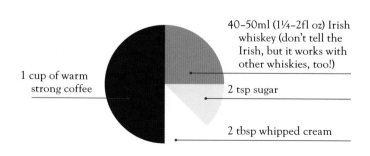

1 cup of warm strong coffee

40–50ml (1¼–2fl oz) Irish whiskey (don't tell the Irish, but it works with other whiskies, too!)

2 tsp sugar

2 tbsp whipped cream

RECIPE

01 Pour the whiskey, sugar and hot coffee into the cup.

02 Stir to dissolve the sugar.

03 Float the whipped cream over the back of a warm spoon so that it doesn't mix with the drink.

04 Dust with freshly grated nutmeg and/or grated chocolate, if desired.

THE OLD FASHIONED

If you were a fan of the TV series *Mad Men*, then you'll have heard Don Draper order an old fashioned on more than one occasion.

HISTORY

The old fashioned is said to have its roots in Louisville, Kentucky, with the earliest records dating back to 1881. A bartender at the Pendennis Club in Louisville invented the old fashioned whiskey cocktail to pay tribute to Colonel James E. Pepper, owner of a bourbon distillery.

The wealthy and well-connected Pepper was such a fan of the old fashioned that he ordered one in all the towns he visited during his subsequent business trips, including at the famous Waldorf-Astoria Hotel in New York. The old fashioned 'went viral,' as we might say today, and soon everyone was drinking it. It even gave its name to the glass that it was served in.

During Prohibition the cocktail went undercover, with bartenders discretely adding sparkling water and lemon zest to disguise the taste of alcohol.

INGREDIENTS

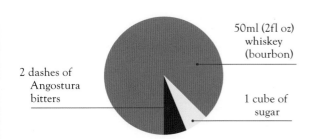

2 dashes of Angostura bitters

50ml (2fl oz) whiskey (bourbon)

1 cube of sugar

RECIPE

Preparing a genuine old fashioned is simple.

01 Put the sugar cube in the glass, add the Angostura bitters and a few drops of whiskey.

02 Stir vigorously with a spoon until the sugar is fully dissolved.

03 Add ice and the remaining whiskey.

04 Add a slice of orange and a maraschino cherry for decoration.

THE MANHATTAN

In the USA, in New York, to be exact, things are generally humming on the cocktail scene, and classic cocktails are no exception. The Manhattan is one of those rare drinks that mixes whisky successfully with another type of alcohol – in this case, red vermouth.

HISTORY

As usual, there are plenty of stories surrounding the origin of the Manhattan. One of these links the name to New York's Manhattan Club, where it is claimed the drink was invented in 1874 at the request of Lady Randolph Churchill (who was about to give birth to a son, Winston, the future British prime minister). The Churchill link is doubtful, as she was in Britain at the time, but The Manhattan Club connection may be true.

An alternative story concerns a Supreme Court justice, Charles Henry Truaux, who was a heavy drinker of martinis and wanted to lose weight. He asked a bartender to prepare a less-calorific cocktail, and the Manhattan was born, using whisky instead! Whether Truaux slimmed down, we will never know.

INGREDIENTS

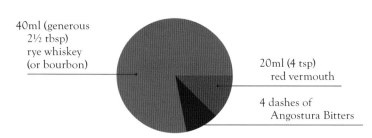

40ml (generous 2½ tbsp) rye whiskey (or bourbon)

20ml (4 tsp) red vermouth

4 dashes of Angostura Bitters

RECIPE

Use a mixing glass

01 Stir all the ingredients together.

02 Add ice.

03 Stir with a bar spoon.

04 Pour into a martini glass, holding back the ice.

05 Garnish with a maraschino cherry.

MINT JULEP

The mint julep is the ultimate cooling, refreshing cocktail. What's more, it's simple to make. The container is as important as the cocktail, and it is traditionally served in a silver julep cup. So say goodbye to those mojitos: it's time for a mint julep.

HISTORY

The mint julep dates back to a Persian drink originating from the year 400, called a *julab*. This drink contained no alcohol, but was made with water, sugar, honey and fruits, and it was used for medicinal purposes.

By the 18th century, the julab had evolved over many centuries to become an alcoholic drink, the julep, made of mint and distilled alcohol.

The first written record of the cocktail comes from Virginia in 1787, where it is described as being made with Cognac or rum. It would be another hundred years before these spirits would be replaced by whiskey.

GEORGES' TIP

Prepare the mixture of mint, syrup and bitters in advance and keep them refrigerated for several hours. The whisky will then be able to soak up the aromas much more effectively.

INGREDIENTS

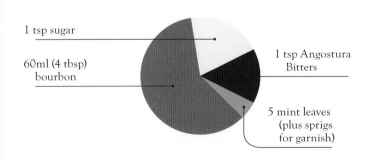

1 tsp sugar

60ml (4 tbsp) bourbon

1 tsp Angostura Bitters

5 mint leaves (plus sprigs for garnish)

RECIPE

Mix directly in the glass – or julep cup if you have one.

01 Place the glass (or cup) in the freezer for 10 minutes before making the cocktail.

02 Remove the stems from the mint, then lightly bruise the mint leaves in a mortar and pestle.

03 Stir the mint, sugar syrup and bitters in the glass.

04 Fill with crushed ice and add the whisky.

05 Stir gently.

06 Garnish with a sprig of mint.

THE WHISKY SOUR

A sour is really easy to prepare: it can be made with pretty much any kind of alcohol (including pisco, brandy, whisky, gin or rum) and uses ingredients that are easy to find: eggs, citrus fruits and sugar.

History

The whisky sour recipe was first published in 1862 in *Jerry Thomas' Bar-Tenders Guide*. But the basic recipe had already been around for more than a century, and its origins come from seafaring. In those days, travel by sea meant spending weeks, or even months, onboard ship, with no refrigeration and often only limited supplies of fresh water. Sailors were entitled to a ration of alcohol (despite its dehydrating properties) and English Vice Admiral Edward Vernon experimented with mixing other ingredients with the alcohol ration to ensure his sailors didn't get drunk. He found that rum could be weakened with lemon or lime juice (kept onboard to prevent scurvy) – and from there, it was just a short step to the whisky sour.

Ingredients

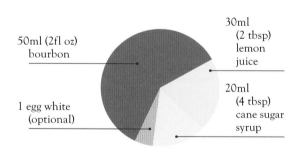

50ml (2fl oz) bourbon

1 egg white (optional)

30ml (2 tbsp) lemon juice

20ml (4 tbsp) cane sugar syrup

The recipe

Prepare in a cocktail shaker.

01 Put ice cubes into a cocktail glass to cool it.

02 Fill two-thirds of the large tumbler of the cocktail shaker with ice cubes.

03 Pour all the ingredients into the small tumbler of the shaker.

04 Empty the ice from the cocktail glass.

05 In the shaker, transfer the ingredients from the small tumbler to the large tumbler. Close the shaker and shake for around 6–10 seconds. Pour the mixture into the cocktail glass, straining out the ice cubes.

06 Garnish with a cocktail cherry, or a slice of lemon or orange on the side of the glass.

07 You can also add few drops of egg white to add smoothness. For this, start with a dry shake (without ice) for the first shake, and then add ice for a second shake. This type of cocktail is sometimes called a Boston sour.

Georges' tip

If you don't have sugar syrup available at home, you can make a quick substitute by diluting white sugar in sparkling water.

SAZERAC

While the original recipe for a Sazerac is made with Cognac,
the whiskey version is what we're naturally looking at here.

HISTORY

It all started in New Orleans, in 1837, when Antoine-
Amédée Peychaud, originally from the former French
colony of Saint-Domingue (now Haiti), bought a drugstore.
He went on to create aromatic bitters, which he marketed
as an invigorating medicine. Peychaud's Bitters was born.

Peychaud then met John B. Shiller, manager of the Sazerac
Coffee House and the New Orleans representative of a
French Cognac distiller called Sazerac de Forge, based in

Limoges, France. Peychaud and Shiller teamed up, putting
Peychaud's bitters with Shiller's Cognac, and the resulting
Cognac Sazerac met with some success. However when
Cognac production was hit by a phylloxera blight near the
end of the 19th century, the Sazerac Coffee House owner
at the time (Thomas Handy) replaced the Cognac with rye
whiskey, thus creating the first whiskey-based Sazerac.

INGREDIENTS

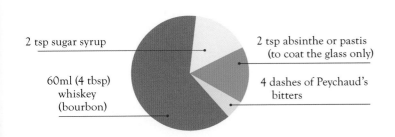

2 tsp sugar syrup

60ml (4 tbsp)
whiskey
(bourbon)

2 tsp absinthe or pastis
(to coat the glass only)

4 dashes of Peychaud's
bitters

RECIPE

Mix directly in the serving glass.

01 Cool the glass with ice cubes, pastis/
absinthe and water.

02 Empty the contents of the glass.

03 Mix all the ingredients in the glass.

04 Add a lemon zest for garnish.

BOURBON-BASED COCKTAILS

AMERICAN PIE MARTINI

Mix ingredients in a cocktail shaker.
Serve in a martini glass.

2½ tbsp bourbon
4 tsp schnapps
4 tsp crème de myrtille (blueberry)
4 tsp cranberry juice
2 tsp apple juice
1 tsp freshly squeezed lime juice

BLACK ROSE

Mix ingredients in a mixing glass.
Serve in a whisky glass.

2 tbsp bourbon
2 tbsp Cognac
2 tsp grenadine syrup
3 dashes of Peychaud's bitters
1 dash of Angostura bitters

BRIGHTON PUNCH

Mix ingredients in a cocktail shaker.
Serve in a collins glass.

50ml (2fl oz) bourbon
50ml (2fl oz) Bénédictine liqueur
50ml (2fl oz) cognac
80ml (2¾fl oz) pineapple juice
60ml (4 tbsp) freshly squeezed
    lemon juice

AMERICANA

Mix ingredients in a chilled glass.
Serve in a flute glass.

1 cube caster (superfine) sugar
4 dashes of Angostura bitters
4 tsp bourbon
top up with Champagne

BLINKER

Mix ingredients in a cocktail shaker.
Serve in a coupe glass.

60ml (4 tbsp) bourbon
2 tsp grenadine syrup
2 tbsp freshly squeezed grapefruit juice

BROOKLYN #1

Mix ingredients in a mixing glass.
Serve in a martini glass.

70ml (2½fl oz) bourbon
2 tsp maraschino liqueur
4 tsp Martini Rosso vermouth
3 dashes of Angostura bitters

AVENUE

Mix ingredients in a cocktail shaker.
Serve in a martini glass.

1 fresh passion fruit
2 tsp bourbon
2 tbsp Calvados
2 tsp grenadine syrup
a few drops of orange flower water
1 dash of Angostura orange bitters
4 tsp chilled mineral water

BLUEGRASS

Mix ingredients in a cocktail shaker.
Serve in a martini glass.

5cm (2in) piece of cucumber peeled,
    cut into pieces and muddled
50ml (2fl oz) bourbon
4 tsp Aperol
a few drops of sugar syrup
1 dash of Angostura orange bitters
1 dash of Angostura aromatic bitters

BROWN DERBY

Mix ingredients in a cocktail shaker.
Serve in a coupe glass.

50ml (2fl oz) bourbon
2 tbsp freshly squeezed pink
    grapefruit juice
2 tsp maple syrup

BOURBON-BASED COCKTAILS

◇◇◇◇◇◇◇◇◇◇◇◇◇◇◇◇◇◇◇◇

DAISY DUKE

Mix ingredients in a cocktail shaker.
Serve in a whisky glass.

60ml (4 tbsp) bourbon
4 tsp grenadine syrup
2 tbsp freshly squeezed lemon juice

FRISCO SOUR

Mix ingredients in a cocktail shaker.
Serve in a whisky glass.

60ml (4 tbsp) bourbon
4 tsp Bénédictine liqueur
4 tsp freshly squeezed lemon juice
2 tsp sugar syrup
½ egg white

MAPLE LEAF

Mix ingredients in a cocktail shaker.
Serve in a whisky glass.

60ml (4 tbsp) bourbon
4 tsp freshly squeezed lemon juice
2 tsp maple syrup

DANDY COCKTAIL

Mix ingredients in a mixing glass.
Serve in a martini glass.

50ml (2fl oz) bourbon
½ tsp triple sec liqueur
50ml (2fl oz) Dubonnet Red
1 dash of Angostura bitters

FRUIT SOUR

Mix ingredients in a cocktail shaker.
Serve in a whisky glass.

2 tbsp bourbon
2 tbsp triple sec liqueur
2 tbsp freshly squeezed lemon juice
4 tsp egg white

MAPLE OLD FASHIONED

Mix ingredients in a mixing glass.
Serve in a martini glass

60ml (4 tbsp) bourbon
4 tsp maple syrup
2 dashes of Angostura bitters

DE LA LOUISIANE

Mix ingredients in a mixing glass.
Serve in a martini glass.

60ml (4 tbsp) bourbon
2 tsp Bénédictine liqueur
4 tsp chilled water
1 dash of Angostura bitters

MAN-BOUR-TINI

Mix ingredients in a cocktail shaker.
Serve in a martini glass.

4 tsp bourbon
2 tbsp Mandarine Napoléon liqueur
4 tsp freshly squeezed lime juice
60ml (4 tbsp) cranberry juice
2 tsp sugar syrup

MOCCA MARTINI

Mix ingredients in a cocktail shaker,
float cream in centre of drink.
Serve in a martini glass.

50ml (2fl oz) bourbon
2 tbsp espresso coffee
    (freshly made and hot)
½ tsp Baileys Irish cream liqueur
½ tsp crème de cacao
½ tsp single cream (to float)

BOURBON-BASED COCKTAILS

RED APPLE

Mix ingredients in a cocktail shaker. Serve in a martini glass.

50ml (2fl oz) bourbon
4 tsp sour apple liqueur
60ml (4 tbsp) cranberry juice

TOAST & ORANGE MARTINI

Mix ingredients in a cocktail shaker. Serve in a martini glass.

60ml (4 tbsp) bourbon
1 tsp orange marmalade
3 dashes of Peychaud's bitters
a few drops of sugar syrup

WALDORF COCKTAIL #1

Mix ingredients in a mixing glass. Serve in a martini glass.

60ml (4 tbsp) bourbon
2 tbsp Martini Rosso vermouth
1 tsp absinthe
2 dashes of Angostura bitters

SHAMROCK #1

Mix ingredients in a mixing glass. Serve in a martini glass.

70ml (2½fl oz) Bourbon
¼ tsp Menthe Verte liqueur
2 tbsp Martini Rosso vermouth
2 dashes of Angostura bitters

VIEW CARRÉ COCKTAIL

Mix ingredients in a mixing glass. Serve in a whisky glass.

2 tbsp bourbon
2 tbsp Cognac
2 tsp Bénédictine liqueur
2 tbsp Martini Rosso vermouth
1 dash of Angostura bitters
1 dash of Peychaud's bitters

WARD EIGHT

Mix ingredients in a cocktail shaker. Serve in a martini glass.

70ml (2½fl oz) bourbon
4 tsp freshly squeezed lemon juice
4 tsp freshly squeezed orange juice
2 tsp grenadine syrup
4 tsp chilled water

SUBURBAN

Mix ingredients in a mixing glass. Serve in a whisky glass.

50ml (2fl oz) bourbon
4 tsp rum
4 tsp tawny port
1 dash of Angostura bitters
1 dash of Angostura orange bitters

VIEUX NAVIRE

Mix ingredients in a mixing glass. Serve in a coupe glass.

2 tbsp bourbon
2 tbsp Calvados
2 tbsp Martini Rosso vermouth
1 dash of Angostura bitters
1 dash of maple bitters

JERRY THOMAS

(1830–1885)

If you're enjoying a good cocktail while reading this book, then you may have to thank Jerry Thomas: one of the pioneers of mixology.

B orn in New York in 1830, Thomas was still a young man when he crossed the continent during the gold rush era to try to make his fortune in California. He had little success in finding gold, but he did find his vocation as a bartender.

Returning to New York in 1921, Thomas became the owner of a saloon based underneath PT Barnum's American Museum. He began to work on every detail of his technique as a bartender, which became more and more extravagant. It became pure showmanship, from his mixing equipment to his flamboyant costumes and the acrobatic ease with which he would juggle mixers, glasses and drinks.

Finding enormous success in New York, he then went on a tour of the country, and later of Europe, where people flocked to see him perform and learn his technique. At the time he was earning more than $100 per week, which was more than the vice-president of the United States.

At age 31, Thomas wrote the first book about alcoholic drinks ever to be published in the USA, called *Jerry Thomas' Bar-Tenders Guide*. While his profession once passed on recipes and techniques orally, Thomas put all this down in print, with recipes both for the classics and for his own creations.

Jerry Thomas was first and foremost a creator, continually coming up with new ideas and new techniques. One of his most famous is the Blue Blazer, in which whisky is ignited and passes from a mixing glass into the serving glass in a great arc of blue flame.

COCKTAILS BASED ON
A BLENDED WHISKY

HONEY & MARMALADE DRAM

Mix ingredients in a mixing glass.
Serve in a martini glass.

60ml (4 tbsp) blended Scotch whisky
4 tsp honey
2 tbsp freshly squeezed lemon juice
2 tbsp freshly squeezed orange juice

GOLD

Mix ingredients in a cocktail shaker.
Serve in a martini glass.

50ml (2fl oz) blended Scotch whisky
2 tbsp triple sec liqueur
2 tbsp banana liqueur
4 tsp chilled water

HOT TODDY

Mix ingredients in a mixing glass.
Serve in a toddy glass.

1 spoon honey
60ml (4 tbsp) blended Scotch whisky
2 tbsp freshly squeezed lemon juice
4 tsp sugar syrup
3 cloves
top up with boiling water

FRENCH WHISKY SOUR

Mix ingredients in a cocktail shaker.
Serve in a whisky glass.

50ml (2fl oz) blended Scotch whisky
1 tbsp Ricard
2 tbsp freshly squeezed lemon juice
1 tbsp sugar syrup
½ egg white
3 dashes of Angostura bitters

HAROLD & MAUDE

Mix ingredients in a cocktail shaker.
Serve in a coupe glass.

50ml (2fl oz) blended Scotch whisky
2 tbsp rum
4 tsp freshly squeezed lemon juice
2 tsp rose syrup
2 tsp lavender syrup

MAMIE TAYLER

Mix ingredients in a mixing glass.
Serve in a collins glass.

60ml (4 tbsp) blended Scotch whisky
2 tsp freshly squeezed lemon juice
top up with ginger ale

GE BLONDE

Mix ingredients in a cocktail shaker.
Serve in a martini glass.

50ml (2fl oz) blended Scotch whisky
2½ tbsp sauvignon blanc white wine
2 tbsp apple juice
2 tsp sugar syrup
2 tsp freshly squeezed lemon juice

HONEY COBBLER

Mix honey and whisky in a mixing glass,
add other ingredients in cocktail shaker.
Serve in a goblet.

2 tsp honey
50ml (2fl oz) blended Scotch whisky
2 tbsp red wine
2 tsp crème de cassis

MANICURE

Mix ingredients in a mixing glass.
Serve in a coupe glass.

2 tbsp Calvados
2 tbsp blended Scotch whisky
2 tbsp Drambuie

COCKTAILS BASED ON A BLENDED WHISKY

~~~~~~

MILK & HONEY MARTINI

Mix ingredients in a cocktail shaker.
Serve in a martini glass.

60ml (4 tbsp) blended Scotch whisky
3 spoonfuls of liquid honey
1 tbsp honey liqueur
4 tsp crème fraiche
4 tsp milk

PAISLEY MARTINI

Mix ingredients in a mixing glass.
Serve in a martini glass.

80ml (2¾fl oz) dry gin
2 tsp blended Scotch whisky
4 tsp extra-dry vermouth

PINEAPPLE BLOSSOM

Mix ingredients in a cocktail shaker.
Serve in a martini glass.

60ml (4 tbsp) blended Scotch whisky
2 tbsp pineapple juice
4 tsp freshly squeezed lemon juice
4 tsp sugar syrup

MORNING GLORY FIZZ

Mix ingredients in a cocktail shaker.
Serve in a collins glass.

60ml (4 tbsp) blended Scotch whisky
4 tsp freshly squeezed lemon juice
4 tsp sugar syrup
½ egg white
1 dash of absinthe
top up with sparkling water

PEAR SHAPED #2

Mix ingredients in a cocktail shaker.
Serve in a collins glass.

60ml (4 tbsp) blended Scotch whisky
2 tbsp Cognac
90ml (3fl oz) apple juice
4 tsp freshly squeezed lime juice
2 tsp vanilla sugar syrup

SCOTCH MILK PUNCH

Mix ingredients in a cocktail shaker.
Serve in a martini glass.

60ml (4 tbsp) blended Scotch whisky
2 tsp sugar syrup
4 tsp single (light) cream
2 tbsp milk

SCOTCH NEGRONI

Mix ingredients in a mixing glass.
Serve in a whisky glass.

2 tbsp blended Scotch whisky
2 tbsp Campari
2 tbsp red vermouth

COCKTAILS WITH SINGLE MALT

AMBER NECTAR

Mix ingredients in a mixing glass. Serve in a coupe glass.

60ml (4 tbsp) single malt
2 tsp peated single malt whisky
2 tsp honey
2 tbsp extra-dry vermouth

MIDTOWN MUSE

Mix ingredients in a mixing glass. Serve in a martini glass.

2½ tbsp single malt
4 tsp melon liqueur
4 tsp Licor 43 (a lightly spiced
   vanilla liqueur)
1 dash of Angostura bitters
4 tsp chilled water

WHISKY BUTTER

Mix ingredients in a cocktail shaker. Serve in a martini glass.

2½ tbsp blended Scotch whisky
4 tsp fino sherry
2 tsp yellow Chartreuse
4 tsp advocaat
2 tsp peated single malt,
   to float on surface of drink

DANTES IN FERNET

Mix ingredients in a cocktail shaker. Serve in a coupe glass.

2 tbsp single malt
60ml (4 tbsp) Fernet-Branca
2 tbsp blood-orange juice
2 tsp maple syrup
1 dash of Bittermens Xocolatl Mole bitters

COCKTAILS WITH BAILEYS

ABSINTHE WITHOUT LEAVE

Layer the ingredients. Serve in a shot glass.

4 tsp Pisang Ambon
4 tsp Baileys
2 tsp absinthe

B52 SHOT

Layer the ingredients. Serve in a shot glass.

4 tsp coffee liqueur
4 tsp Baileys
4 tsp Grand Marnier

APACHE

Layer the ingredients. Serve in a shot glass.

4 tsp coffee liqueur
2 tsp melon liqueur
2 tsp Baileys

LEMON MERINGUE MARTINI

Mix ingredients in a cocktail shaker. Serve in a martini glass.

60ml (4 tbsp) vodka
2 tbsp Baileys
2 tbsp freshly squeezed lemon juice
2 tsp sugar syrup

CHOCOLATE & MINT MARTINI

Mix ingredients in a mixing glass. Serve in a martini glass.

60ml (4 tbsp) vodka
4 tsp white chocolate liqueur
4 tsp Baileys
4 tsp hazelnut liqueur
4 tsp black raspberry liqueur
4 tsp single (light) cream
4 tsp milk

 GEORGES' LAYERING TIP

When a recipe asks you to prepare the ingredients in layers, this means pouring the ingredients into the cocktail one after another, running them gently down the length of the mixing spoon so that they remain in horizontal layers without mixing. Take it slowly!

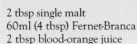

JOHN WALKER

(1805–1857)

You guessed it: this is the man behind the famous whisky brand.

John Walker, nicknamed Johnnie, had just turned 14 when his father died. The family sold their farm and used the funds to start a grocery store in Kilmarnock, Scotland. Johnnie had a nose for business, and soon became one of the most respected shopkeepers in town. However, what really interested Johnnie Walker was whisky. At the time, Scottish grocery stores usually kept bottles of single-malt whisky in stock, but Walker found the quality just too variable, so he decided to create his own blends of whisky to control the taste. He even created bespoke blends that suited his various customers.

When he died in 1957, Walker's son, Alexander, took over the business, by which time sales of whisky had outstripped all other products. Alexander continued to build the spirits business. He created a brand name for his most popular blend – Old Highland Whisky – and introduced the famous square bottle, which was more resilient to breakage in transit. He also engaged ships' captains as agents for his whisky, which quickly gave him a growing network of sales almost anywhere with a shipping port: a contributing factor to the eventual worldwide reach of the brand. In 2015, Johnnie Walker was the world's-third biggest-selling whisky.

WHISKY-BASED BEVERAGES

Whisky does not exist in splendid isolation, but forms the base of a growing range of drinks derived from it – each offering its own unique taste.

LIQUEURS

Whisky liqueurs are based on Scotch whisky or Irish whiskey, with the addition of herbs, spices, honey or various other ingredients according to the recipe. They are all generally around 15 per cent ABV, but none are higher than 20 per cent. One of the oldest and best-known whisky liqueurs is Drambuie – the name comes from a Gaelic word meaning 'the drink that satisfies' – which has been in production for more than a hundred years. Its principal ingredients are a blended Scotch and heather honey.

CREAM LIQUEURS

When we think of cream liqueurs, Baileys is the name that most immediately springs to mind, and it is widely sold in almost every supermarket. The brand now belongs to Diageo, owner of Johnnie Walker and J&B (among others). What's the recipe? A mixture of sugar, cream, Irish whiskey and aromatic herbs. There are other cream liqueurs, too, such as Edradour Cream Liqueur, which is based, of course, on Edradour single malt.

WHEN SCOTLAND MET IRELAND

There may be centuries of rivalry between Scottish and Irish distillers, but this drink brings together the two traditions in a single liqueur known as Rusty Mist. Here, Drambuie (from Scotland) is paired with Irish Mist, an Irish whiskey liqueur flavoured with herbs and honey. The latter has its origins in heather wine, a drink traditionally served to Irish clan chiefs.

The distilleries' view

You might think that the distilleries would disapprove of all these whisky spinoffs, seeing them as a departure from whisky purity. Not at all. In fact, they love it. More and more whisky brands are launching their own products, viewing it as a chance to reach new customers and create new methods of tasting whisky's unique flavours.

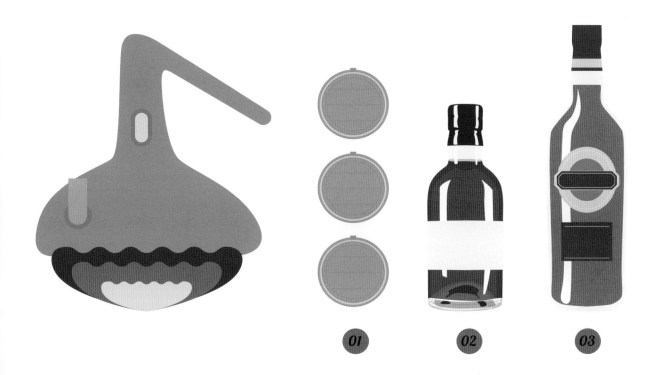

01   **02**   **03**

Flavoured whisky?!

Whisky infused with lime? Or with honey? Or cherries? According to the strict rules of what can or can't go into whisky (only water and sometimes caramel colouring are permitted), these products seem way out of line. However, they are not, strictly speaking, 'whisky'. Instead, they are considered whisky-based 'spirit drinks', and their level of alcohol (at around 35 per cent ABV) is another important differentiating factor.

These drinks have been designed to bring in new consumers who either disliked the taste of whisky or weren't used to it. They also open up new possibilities in the world of cocktails. Many distilleries, not surprisingly, are spending vast sums in their development. And who knows? You may even want to give them a try!

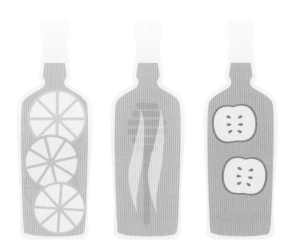

Whisky-based beverages

N⁻6
THE WORLD TOUR

O wning a bottle of whisky is one thing. But knowing where it comes from makes it a bit more special. Where is its distillery located, and what other distilleries are nearby? Knowing that might inspire you to organize a tasting, or to think of other bottles that you might add to your collection, or just to widen your horizons a little further. In any case, it's time to take the world tour.

SCOTLAND

It may seem the obvious place to start, but we can't talk about whisky without talking about Scotland!

THE GIANT OF WHISKY

The numbers say it all: there are more than a hundred active distilleries and two hundred brands of single malt alone (and that's without even counting the blends). The Scotch whisky industry's exports are worth around £4bn ($4.9bn) annually, and the equivalent of 40 bottles of whisky are exported from Scotland every second.

SCOTLAND'S REGIONS

From 1980, the Scotch Whisky Association began to classify whisky according to five distinct regions to help consumers get a better understanding of the differences. There are some parallels with the concept of regional wine (think of Bordeaux and Burgundy, for instance), but there are limits as to how far this comparison goes, especially given that much of the barley used in whisky-making is imported, so takes in nothing from Scottish soil. What is local and distinct, however, is the water, the techniques and the traditions, all of which tend to be specific to a region: Speyside, for example. There are, however, plenty of exceptions, too.

GHOSTS...AND SPIRITS

Scotland is world-renowned for its haunted castles, but if you really want to get goose bumps during a distillery tour, then head to the Glen Scotia Distillery in Campbeltown. Duncan MacCallum, one of the owners, was forced to close the distillery in 1928 and drowned himself in Campbell Loch two years later. According to local legend, his ghost continues to haunt the distillery, which resumed production in 1933.

HIGHLANDS

ISLAY

CAMPBELTOWN

SPEYSIDE

MACALLAN 64YO
SINGLE MALT

LOWLANDS

ANY WHISKY LEFT?

Contrary to a persistent rumour, Scotland's whisky warehouses are still full! More than 20 million casks are currently stacked up, maturing slowly, waiting for bottling. Even so, with demand for whisky currently booming, more and more non-age-statement (NAS – see page 98) whiskies are appearing on the market. While these are all at least three years old, they still allow distilleries to bring new whiskies onto the market more quickly in a bid to satisfy global demand.

THE $460,000 BOTTLE

The most expensive bottle of whisky ever sold went under the hammer at Sotheby's in New York in 2010 for $460,000: it was The Macallan 64YO single malt in a 6-litre (1½-gallon) bespoke Lalique crystal carafe made using the 'lost wax' technique, and measuring 71cm (28in) high – the biggest ever made. All proceeds of the sale went to charity.

FROM JAPAN TO SCOTLAND

Japanese drinks giant Suntory owns three distilleries in Scotland: Auchentoshan, Bowmore and Glen Garioch. Its Japanese rival Nikka owns the Ben Nevis Distillery. Legend has it that a small amount of Scotch is present in certain Japanese blends.

TARTANS

Hard to talk about Scotland without addressing the subject of tartans. You are probably already aware of the Scottish and their tartans, but are perhaps more intrigued by what they wear under their kilt rather than the patterns of the fabric.

WHAT IT IS

Tartan is a woven fabric formed with a striped design running through the warp and the weft of the weave – so both horizontally and vertically – originating in the Highlands of Scotland. It is most often seen in the form of the traditional Scottish kilt.

A BRIEF HISTORY

The earliest tartan can be traced back to 1538 in Scotland. By around 1700, tartans were being used to identify the inhabitants of different districts. Following the failed uprising of Charles Edward Stuart (aka Bonnie Prince Charlie), the English invaded Scotland, and in 1747 banned the wearing of tartan. However, the fabric began to reappear towards 1820, thanks to the records kept over decades by various weavers. By the end of the 19th century all Scottish clans had reclaimed their distinctive tartan signatures.

WHAT YOUR TARTAN SAYS ABOUT YOU

According to legend, you can tell a lot about someone based simply on the tartan they wear:
* One colour for servants;
* Two colours for rent-paying farmers;
* Three colours for officers;
* Five colours for chieftains;
* Six for druids and poets;
* Seven for kings;
* And for soldiers at war, red tartans.

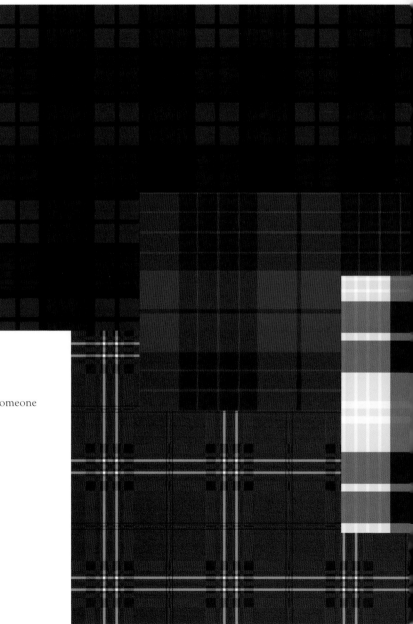

Tartans and kilts

Mention a kilt, and talk will inevitably come round to the question: what do people wear underneath? The answer is simple and unambiguous, and can be found in the ancient regulations of the Scottish army: you wear nothing underneath. If you do intend to wear a kilt during your whisky tastings, don't forget your *sgian dubh*: the small dagger that slips into your right sock. Useful if you need to cut the sealing wax from a bottle of Maker's Mark!

It's a serious business

As with any commercial brand, tartan designs are protected, in this case, by the Scottish Register of Tartans. You can, however, create your own tartan motif, submit it for approval and live your life like a modern-day clan chief.

Speaking of clans...

Traditional Scottish society functioned around clans, where membership was evident by the surname as well as by the distinctive clan tartan on the kilt. The clan chieftain had absolute authority, and ruled on all aspects of the clan's life – including alliances and wars.

Tartans and punks

British punk fashion made much of tartan during the 1970s, perhaps viewing it as a way of appropriating what was once a symbol of power and authority – in Scotland, at least.

North America's tartan day

Tartan Day is an annual festival of Scottish heritage in North America, held on 6 April, the anniversary of the Declaration of Arbroath in 1320 (the independence of Scotland). It demonstrates the close links between Scotland and the wider community of Scots scattered across the continent.

ISLAY

◇◇◇◇◇◇◇◇◇◇

This tiny island is world-renowned for its whisky, which has become an integral part of its identity.

HISTORY

According to some sources, it all started right here. The entire history of whisky may have begun when the Mac Beatha family landed on Islay and brought with them their technique of distillation. Legend has it that their descendants, who became doctors serving the lairds, went on to invent *uisge beatha* (see page 12): the direct ancestor of today's whisky.

THE ISLE OF JURA – AND ANOTHER GEORGE

To reach the neighbouring island of Jura, you have to take a boat from Port Askeig on Islay. On arrival, a single-lane road (with occasional passing places) leads to one distillery and a single hotel. The island has a population of just 200 people, but around 6,000 deer live there, too. Running a distillery in such a remote location is quite a feat. And although it has nothing to do with whisky, author George Orwell wrote his famous novel *1984* here.

GEOGRAPHY

Situated 27km (17 miles) from the Scottish mainland, this tiny island of just 3,000 inhabitants is crossed by four small rivers, and is home to eight distilleries and a malting facility. More than a quarter of the surface area of this windswept isle is made up of peat bog, but it also has areas where barley grows successfully. Despite the wide-scale development of tourism around its distilleries, Islay remains a place of great natural beauty, and promises a genuinely warm welcome to visitors.

TASTE

Peat is a major part of the flavour spectrum for most Islay whiskies, although it has a slightly different tang to the peat found on the mainland, due to a type of moss that is specific to Islay. The island is also home to the most-peated whisky in the world: the famous Octomore from the Bruichladdich Distillery on the west of the island. Not all Islay whiskies are peated, however. Both Bruichladdich and Bunnahabhain also make whiskies with little or no peatiness.

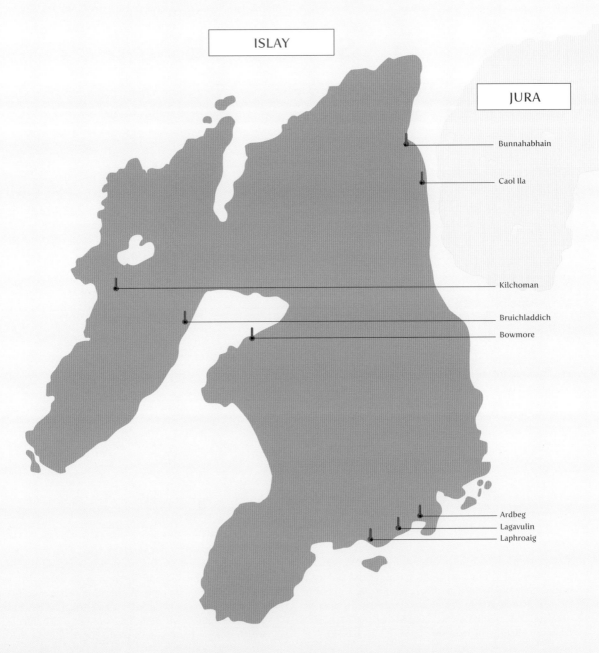

ISLAY

JURA

Bunnahabhain

Caol Ila

Kilchoman

Bruichladdich

Bowmore

Ardbeg
Lagavulin
Laphroaig

GETTING THERE

To really appreciate your pilgrimage to Islay, you'll need to think carefully about travel arrangements. There is an airport on the island with flights to and from Glasgow, but simply flying in will deprive you of part of the magic of the trip. One of the best ways to get there is via train from Glasgow to Oban, which offers breathtaking scenery on the way, then use an air-taxi service, flying over the islands of Jura and Islay before landing on Islay itself. The other option is to take the ferry, which will give you a first glimpse of the distilleries from the sea.

SPEYSIDE

Sometimes called 'the golden triangle of whisky', Speyside is the nerve centre of Scotch whisky production, right in the heart of the Highlands. Nowhere else in the world will you find such a concentration of distilleries within such a small geographical area.

History

Between the wilderness of the mountains and the deeply forested foothills, the region picked up a reputation as an ideal hideout for anyone seeking to escape the forces of law. At the start of the 19th century, various legal constraints governing the sale and production of alcohol meant that many locals set up illegal distilleries in the region, often with local authorities turning a blind eye.

Taste

You may sometimes hear people talking about a 'typical Speyside whisky', which generally means round and mellow, while still being complex and rich, with fruity and floral aromas. Mind you, this is a generalization, and plenty of Speyside distilleries are working to distance themselves from this slightly clichéd view of the region's whisky.

Geography

Speyside lies within the Moray district of Scotland, bordered by the Cairngorm Mountains to the south and the rivers Findhorn to the west and Deveron to the east, with the Moray Firth to the north. Within this area is everything a distiller needs to make great whisky: no fewer than four rivers running down from the mountains; rich, fertile soil in which to grow barley; and a fresh, humid climate that's ideal for ageing casks.

Did you know?

Some of the casks used to create some of the world's most popular blended whisky (such as J&B, Clan Campbell or Johnnie Walker) come from Speyside distilleries.

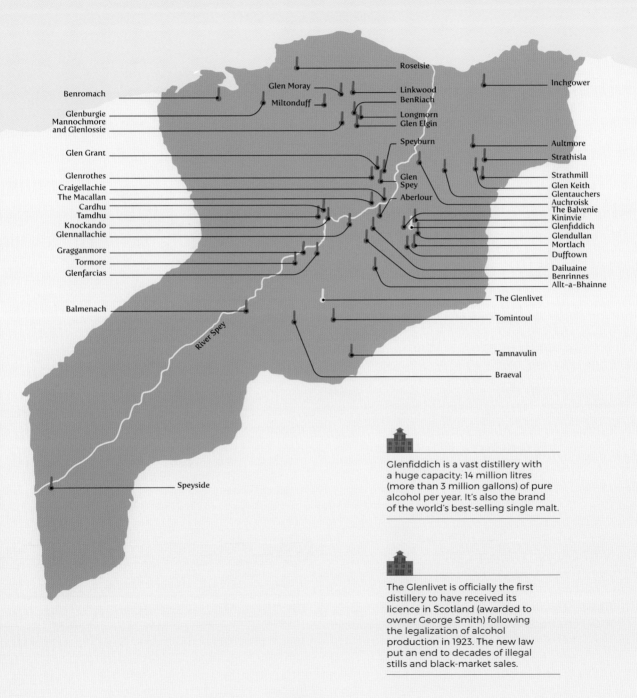

SPEYSIDE

Roseisie

Benromach

Glen Moray

Miltonduff

Linkwood
BenRiach

Inchgower

Glenburgie
Mannochmore
and Glenlossie

Longmorn
Glen Elgin

Glen Grant

Speyburn

Aultmore
Strathisla

Glenrothes
Craigellachie
The Macallan
Cardhu
Tamdhu
Knockando
Glennallachie

Glen
Spey

Aberlour

Strathmill
Glen Keith
Glentauchers
Auchroisk
The Balvenie
Kininvie
Glenfiddich
Glendullan
Mortlach
Dufftown

Gragganmore
Tormore
Glenfarcias

Dailuaine
Benrinnes
Allt-a-Bhainne

Balmenach

The Glenlivet

Tomintoul

River Spey

Tamnavulin

Braeval

Speyside

Glenfiddich is a vast distillery with a huge capacity: 14 million litres (more than 3 million gallons) of pure alcohol per year. It's also the brand of the world's best-selling single malt.

The Glenlivet is officially the first distillery to have received its licence in Scotland (awarded to owner George Smith) following the legalization of alcohol production in 1923. The new law put an end to decades of illegal stills and black-market sales.

THE LOWLANDS

◇◇◇◇◇◇◇◇◇◇◇◇◇◇◇◇◇◇◇◇◇◇◇◇◇◇◇◇◇◇

The Scottish Lowlands are densely populated – although not with distilleries. The reason? Its geographical situation, squeezed between England to the south and the Highlands to the north.

HISTORY

In the second half of the 18th century, Lowland distillers were having a tough time. The Highland Line (separating the Highlands from the Lowlands) literally cut Scotland in two, giving lower tax rates to the Highlands, but a host of tax and other measures that appeared to penalize the Lowland distilleries. To compensate for this, many Lowland distilleries tried to boost production by creating low-quality spirits that were then sold into England to make gin. English distillers were unhappy with this, and eventually the Lowland Licence Act obliged distilleries to give 12 months' notice of any exports to England. The result? The majority of Lowland distilleries went bust within the year.

GEOGRAPHY

Around 80 per cent of Scotland's population lives in the Lowlands, including within its two largest cities, Edinburgh and Glasgow. Yet this is also a fertile region for growing barley and wheat.

 GRAIN DISTILLERIES

The Lowlands is also where you'll find six of Scotland's seven grain distilleries, producing enormous quantities of grain whisky. Much of the vast output goes to make blends.

TASTE

Lowland whiskies are generally rather dry and light, with floral and herbal notes.

Daftmill

Cameronbridge

Auchentoshan

North British

Strathclyde

Edinburgh

Glenkinchie

Glasgow

Girvan
Ailsa Bay

Gretna

Bladnoch

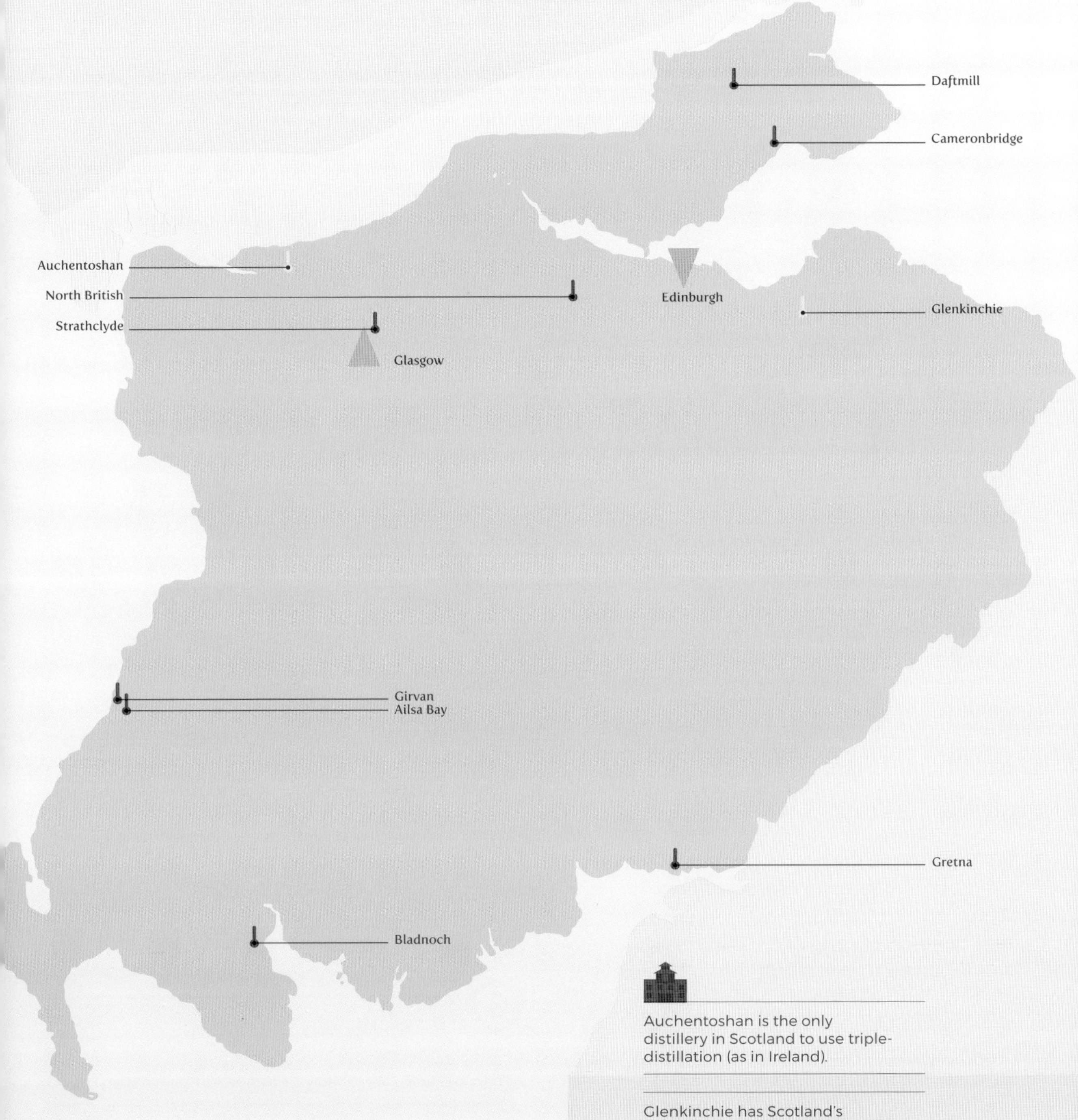

Auchentoshan is the only distillery in Scotland to use triple-distillation (as in Ireland).

Glenkinchie has Scotland's biggest wash still, with a capacity of 32,000 litres (7,039 gallons).

THE HIGHLANDS

The Highlands are Scotland's wilderness – and a whisky tourist's dream – with lochs, castles, unspoiled landscapes, and distilleries aplenty.

HISTORY

The Highlands have always existed on the margins of the rest of Scotland. In the 16th century, they were seen as rebel provinces that needed to be subdued on a regular basis. It was also in the Scottish Highlands that the reformation of the Scottish church took longest, as its population was unwilling to abandon the Roman church. And finally, through all the major national and global conflicts, it is often this region that supplies the greatest number of troops.

GEOGRAPHY

The Highlands includes all of Scotland above the Highland Line, with the exception of Speyside (and the Islands). The region is mountainous, with some peaks exceeding 1,000m (3,281ft); the highest is Ben Nevis at 1,344m (4,410ft).

TASTE

With distilleries spread across a vast area, it's hard to sum up a characteristic taste for Highland whisky. Some have tried to divide it into four or five zones (north, south, east, west and central), while others have tried a three-way split into north, central and eastern. Here is a rough division: the southern Highlands produce single malts that are light and fruity, while those in the west tend to be fruity and spicy.

 | DID YOU KNOW?

In the *Harry Potter* films, the *Hogwarts Express* travels over the famous curved Glenfinnan Viaduct in the western Highlands.

Glenmorangie has resumed its 'designer casks' project, that is, whisky aged in bespoke casks to complement each whisky's specific ideal ageing time.

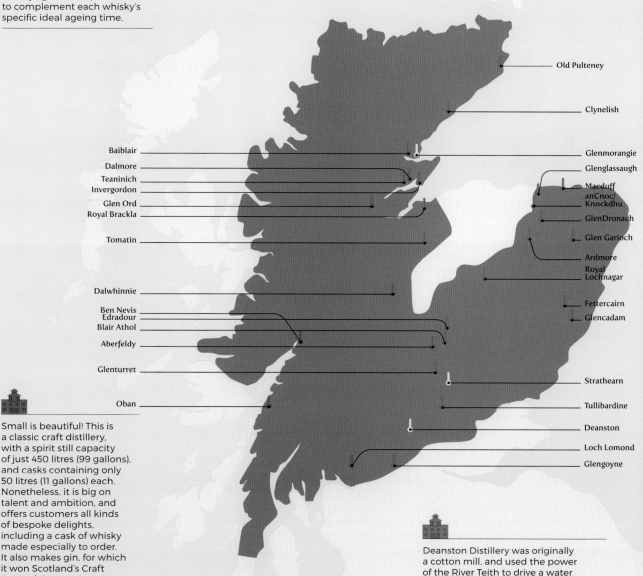

Old Pulteney

Clynelish

Baiblair
Dalmore
Teaninich
Invergordon
Glen Ord
Royal Brackla
Tomatin

Glenmorangie
Glenglassaugh
Macduff
anCnoc/
Knockdhu
GlenDronach
Glen Garioch
Ardmore
Royal Lochnagar

Dalwhinnie

Ben Nevis
Edradour
Blair Athol
Aberfeldy

Glenturret

Oban

Fettercairn
Glencadam

Strathearn

Tullibardine

Deanston

Loch Lomond

Glengoyne

Small is beautiful! This is a classic craft distillery, with a spirit still capacity of just 450 litres (99 gallons), and casks containing only 50 litres (11 gallons) each. Nonetheless, it is big on talent and ambition, and offers customers all kinds of bespoke delights, including a cask of whisky made especially to order. It also makes gin, for which it won Scotland's Craft Spirit of the Year in 2015.

Deanston Distillery was originally a cotton mill, and used the power of the River Teith to drive a water wheel for operating machinery. Today, the wheel has been replaced by more efficient hydraulic turbines that generate enough electricity to power the distillery. Any unused power is sold back into the National Grid.

CAMPBELTOWN

◇◇◇◇◇◇◇◇◇◇◇◇◇◇◇◇◇◇◇◇◇◇◇◇◇◇◇◇◇◇◇◇◇◇◇◇

Once known as 'The Whisky Capital of The World', Campbeltown has faced mixed fortunes. It now has just a handful of distilleries.

HISTORY

At the end of the 19th century it all looked very promising for Campbeltown, a Highland fishing port that also had around 20 distilleries to its name. Steamboats were packing the port, loading up with thousands of whisky casks bound for Glasgow, London and New York. But by the start of the 20th century, Cambeltown's oily/smoky taste had fallen out of fashion, both with the public and with the blenders. Added to this came the Great Depression and the closure of the coalmine, and the result was that the majority of the medium-sized distilleries were forced to quit.

TASTE

With its provenance as a fishing port and its unique taste with its notes of oil and smoke, detractors were quick to denounce Campbeltown's whisky as tasting of 'stinking fish', adding to the general mood of antipathy, with stories of it being matured in barrels that had once contained herring. It was all false, of course, but such rumours helped finish off a local industry that was already on its knees.

GEOGRAPHY

Campbeltown is not a region of Scotland, but simply a fishing port on the extreme west coast. The location is so isolated that it had become customary in Campbeltown to say that the nearest town is in Ireland.

Its earlier history of prosperity gave Campbeltown a special place in the world of whisky. Everything was at hand: a deep-water port to import grain and export whisky, as well as a local coalmine and several maltings.

Today, with just three surviving distilleries, Campbeltown is the smallest Scotch-whisky-producing area of all.

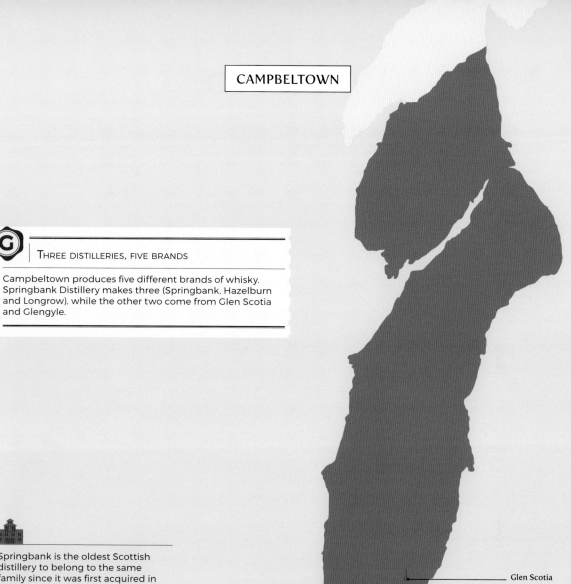

CAMPBELTOWN

Campbeltown produces five different brands of whisky. Springbank Distillery makes three (Springbank, Hazelburn and Longrow), while the other two come from Glen Scotia and Glengyle.

Springbank is the oldest Scottish distillery to belong to the same family since it was first acquired in 1825. Today, the fifth generation of the Mitchell family holds the keys. It's also one of the few Scottish distilleries to carry out the entire whisky production process on site.

Glen Scotia

Glengyle

Springbank

IRELAND

◇◇◇◇◇◇◇◇◇◇◇◇◇◇◇◇◇

Despite its status (along with Scotland) as the birthplace of whiskey/whisky, Ireland has seen a steady decline in whiskey production over the last 200 years.

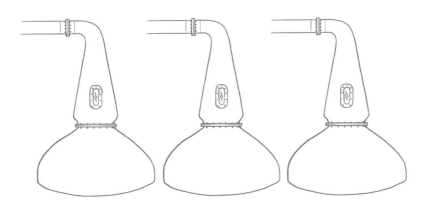

HISTORY

By the end of the 18th century, whiskey was a booming business in Ireland, with more than 2,000 distilleries in operation. Each city had several distilleries, and the Irish triple-pot stills produced fine spirits of high quality, shipped globally from the port of Dublin. The remarkable success of John Jameson (1740–1823) and his descendants created something of a whisky dynasty in the country during the 19th century. Much of the rest of the industry, however, was decimated by a trade war with Britain, which effectively locked Ireland out of lucrative commonwealth countries, such as Canada. This in turn prevented Ireland from supplying the US market across the Canadian border during the Prohibition era, leaving the entire US (illegal) market open to the Scotch producers. By 1930, only six distilleries remained in Ireland, and in 1960 the remaining three merged to create Irish Distillers.

THE PURE POT STILL

The Irish technique of choice starts with the grains, with a 50:50 mix of malted and unmalted barley (originally combined to reduce the excise bill). The resulting wash is triple-distilled in pot stills.

TASTE

The absence of peat and its production method make Irish whiskey typically light and fruity.

POITÍN: STRONG STUFF

Let's not confuse Irish whiskey with *poitín* (sometimes anglicized as poteen), a traditional Irish distilled liquor also based on malted barley (although it can be made with potato starch). Poitín has a very high alcohol content of between 60–95 per cent ABV. Long banned, for decades it was made in illegal stills and finally became legal to buy in 1997, with the poitín name protected by EU law.

IRELAND

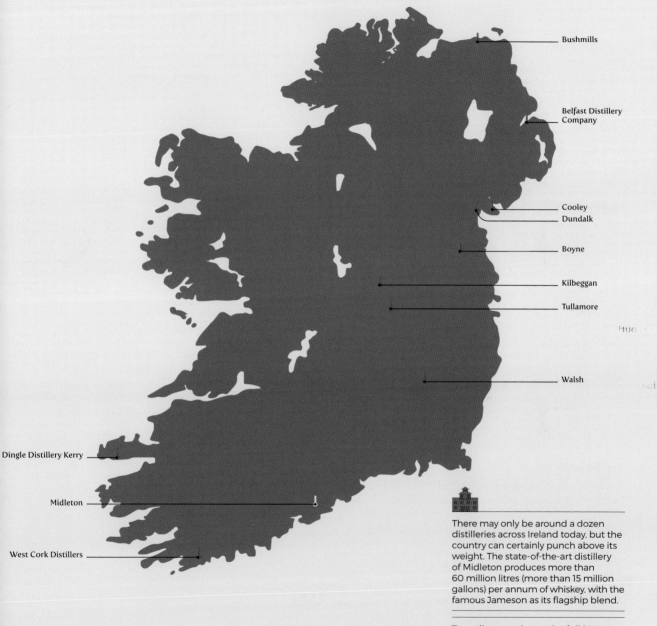

Bushmills

Belfast Distillery Company

Cooley
Dundalk

Boyne

Kilbeggan

Tullamore

Walsh

Dingle Distillery Kerry

Midleton

West Cork Distillers

There may only be around a dozen distilleries across Ireland today, but the country can certainly punch above its weight. The state-of-the-art distillery of Midleton produces more than 60 million litres (more than 15 million gallons) per annum of whiskey, with the famous Jameson as its flagship blend.

To really get to know the full history of Irish whiskey, a visit to the Jameson Distillery on Bow Street, Dublin, is a great place to start. Its museum provides a fascinating walk through distilling history – and the tour finishes, naturally, with a tasting.

THE REST OF THE UNITED KINGDOM

A tour of the United Kingdom wouldn't be complete without a trip to Wales and England.

WALES

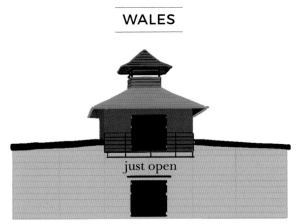

just open

ENGLAND

HISTORY

Just a handful of small distilleries are found in Wales. The oldest, Penderyn Whisky, was launched in 2004, situated on the southern edge of the Brecon Beacons National Park. Its annual production is smaller than the daily output of some of the big distilleries. Unusually, it marks the date of bottling on every single bottle, which can reveal the slight differences that may exist between bottlings.

THE FARADAY STILL

Penderyn uses a single pot still, designed by Dr David Faraday, a descendant of Victorian scientist Michael Faraday. Vapour runs through perforated plates inside a copper column, allowing different types of alcohol to be drawn off.

HISTORY

Having a big reputation as the 'spiritual' home of gin does not make it easy to build a name in the whisky business. However, a few whisky distilleries are active in England, including one in the heart of the capital: The London Distillery Company. Not that this is an entirely new thing. England already had four distilleries by the end of the 19th century, so English whisky, perhaps, is making a comeback.

 | A STORY OF SHENANIGANS

Wales was actually producing whisky in the 19th century – well, sort of. A distillery owner had acquired a still, but rather than go to the trouble of having to operate it, he preferred to buy in alcohol from Scotland, throw in a few spices, and sell them on as Welsh whiskies. When the story got out, the 'distillery' was forced to close down.

 | THE QUEEN'S CORGI

According to press reports from 1999, a disgruntled footman at Buckingham Palace put whisky into the water bowl used by one of the queen's corgis, and the dog fell seriously ill and later died from alcohol poisoning. The queen was said to be furious, and the servant was demoted.

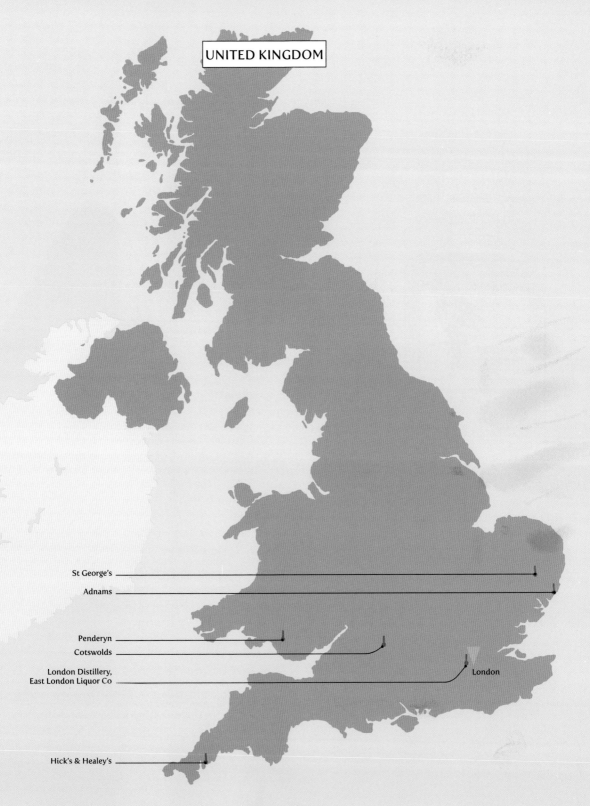

UNITED KINGDOM

St George's

Adnams

Penderyn

Cotswolds

London Distillery,
East London Liquor Co

London

Hick's & Healey's

The rest of the United Kingdom

JAPAN

<><><><><><><><>

*At first they were dismissed as providing no more than a good copy of existing Scotch.
But as time moved on, the inspiration and creativity of Japanese distillers has put them
firmly in the top ranks of world whisky producers.*

HISTORY

When we look at the international
success of Japanese whisky today, it's
hard to believe that whisky production
began less than a hundred years ago.
Japan's first distillery was built in 1923,
in the Kyoto suburb of Yamazaki,
the result of a collaboration between
Shinjiro Torii and Masataka Taketsuru,
men who each went on to create rival
whisky empires – Torii became the man
behind Suntory, while Taketsuru built
Nikka. Today, these two distilleries
remain the major producers of whisky
in Japan, and compete fiercely with
one another – with none of the
collaboration that can sometimes be
found among Scotch producers.

THE FIRST JAPANESE DISTILLERY

It is often claimed that Masataka Taketsuru located his Yamazaki distillery
at Shimamoto because the climate closely resembled that of the Highlands of
Scotland. This is partly true, but much more significant is the availability of water,
thanks to three rivers in close proximity. And not just any rivers. The water is
so famous for its quality that legendary tea-master Sen no Rikyu built his first
Tea House there.

TASTE

Japanese whiskies differ from Scotch mainly through their absence of
any cereal notes. Both Torii and Taketsuru took a scientific research-
based approach to whisky production, in complete contrast to the craft-
style approach taken by Scottish distillers in the 20th century.

BILL MURRAY: JAPANESE WHISKY AMBASSADOR

In the movie *Lost in Translation* by Sofia Coppola. Bill Murray plays an ageing star
staying in Tokyo to film a whisky commercial for Hibiki, a real-life blend belonging
to Suntory. The success of the film was such that it brought a new passion for
Japanese whisky to global markets.

JAPAN

In August 2015, Japanese drinks giant Suntory sent whisky to the International Space Station as part of an experiment to test the impact of zero gravity on the taste. After three years in orbit, the whisky returned, and is now being analysed to understand the results. Despite the existence of Ballantine's zero-gravity whisky glass (see page 71), the astronauts weren't allowed to drink a single drop during the experiment.

Yoichi

Miyagikyo

Karuizawa

Chichibu

Fuji-Gotemba

Yamazaki

Eigashima

THE UNITED STATES

Bourbon, rye, Tennessee whiskey: the USA is a country where whiskey is all about variety and innovation.

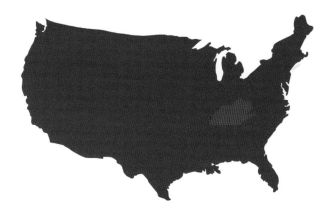

HISTORY

The beginnings of American whiskey can be traced back to the first European settlers, lured in to farm American soil with the offer of a plot of land for growing corn (maize). But with the price of corn too low, many turned to distilling liquor to get a better return for their efforts.

The Industrial Revolution in the middle of the 19th century allowed whiskey production to expand, making use of the new railway networks to find bigger markets. But the growth in the whiskey trade came to an abrupt halt with the intervention of the anti-drinking or 'temperance' movements, and later by Prohibition, which boosted both moonshine distilleries and illegal imports.

KENTUCKY *VS* TENNESSEE

Kentucky is the birthplace of bourbon. Although today bourbon can legally be made anywhere in the USA, this is definitely where it all started.

As for Tennessee whiskey, its uniqueness comes from what's known as the 'Lincoln County Process', which involves filtering the whiskey through sugar-maple charcoal chips. Typically, maple wood is turned into charcoal, and then the whiskey is run through a sizeable charcoal filter some 3m (10ft) high. Once aged in new American oak casks, the result is a bourbon-like whiskey that is both original and soft.

 THE MICRO-DISTILLERY PHENOMENON

Not a week goes by in the USA without news of another start-up bourbon micro-distillery. With as many styles as there are micro-distilleries, bourbon fans are going to be in for a treat.

 JACK DANIEL'S: DON'T EXPECT A TASTING

If you're keen to visit the distillery in Lynchburg, be aware that there will be no tasting at the end of your guided visit. The same applies in all the bars in town. Lynchburg is one of several 'dry cities' in the United States where the sale of any kind of alcoholic beverages is strictly forbidden.

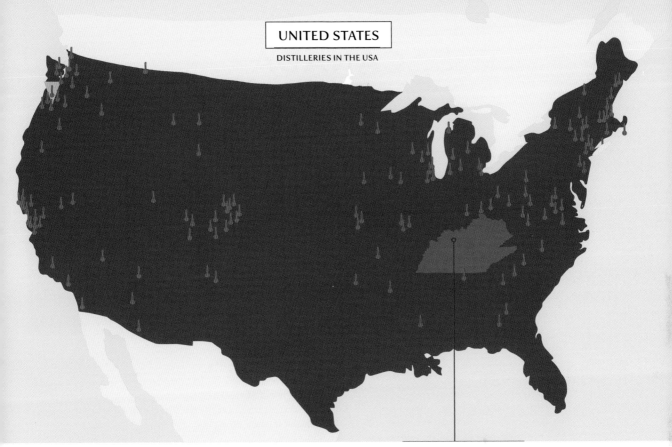

UNITED STATES

DISTILLERIES IN THE USA

DISTILLERIES IN KENTUCKY AND
TENNESSEE

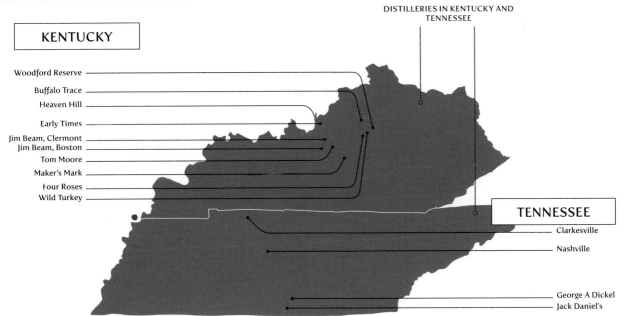

KENTUCKY

Woodford Reserve
Buffalo Trace
Heaven Hill
Early Times
Jim Beam, Clermont
Jim Beam, Boston
Tom Moore
Maker's Mark
Four Roses
Wild Turkey

TENNESSEE

Clarkesville
Nashville

George A Dickel
Jack Daniel's

CANADA

This giant whisky producer, second-largest in volume terms after Scotland, is one of the most low-key players on the global market.

HISTORY

The history of Canadian whisky is closely tied to that of American whiskey. Production in Canada took off during the Prohibition era in the USA; with no supplies from US distilleries, smugglers crossed the Canadian border to buy crates of Canadian spirits. One of the most well-known distilleries is Hiram Walker, based in Windsor, on the Canadian side of the Detroit River just across from the city of the same name. A regular customer during the 1930s was notorious gangster Al Capone.

CANADIAN RYE VS RYE

Nothing is straightforward in the world of whisky. Canadian whisky is called rye whisky, but may contain little or no rye. And it tastes nothing like American rye whiskey, which actually *is* based on a mash containing 51 per cent rye. Got that?

Historically, Canadian whisky was in fact made mainly with rye, as it grew well in the arable lands in Canada's eastern territories. These days, the use of rye in Canadian whisky is less current, given that the more fertile terrains of western Canada produce plenty of alternative cereals. Nonetheless, the name of Canadian Rye lives on.

TASTE

Canadian whiskies often contain notes of cinnamon, toasted bread or caramel.

Ⓖ | VALUE FOR MONEY

Don't think for one moment that the low-ish prices of Canadian whiskies mean the quality may be in any way compromised or substandard. On the contrary, most provide excellent value for money.

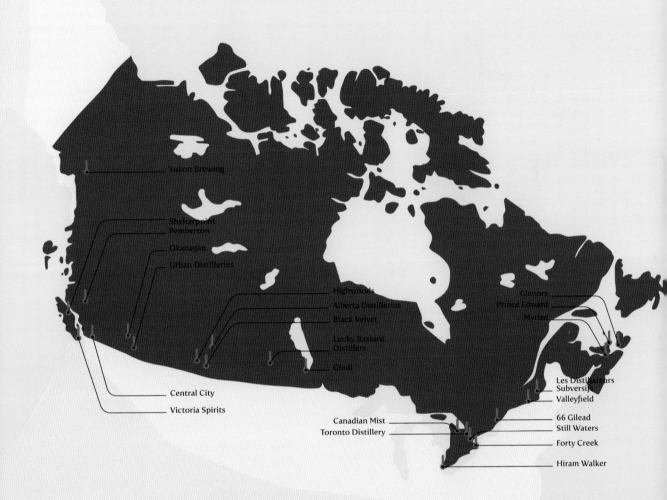

Yukon Brewing

Shelterpoint
Pemberton

Okanagan

Urban Distilleries

Highwoods

Alberta Distilleries

Black Velvet

Lucky Bastard
Distillers

Gimli

Central City

Victoria Spirits

Glenora

Prince Edward

Myriad

Les Distillateurs
Subversifs

Valleyfield

Canadian Mist

Toronto Distillery

66 Gilead

Still Waters

Forty Creek

Hiram Walker

Canadians love eggnog, also known
as milk punch or, in French-speaking
Canada, *lait de poulet* (literally
translated: 'chicken milk'). This dairy-
based beverage is traditionally made
with milk, eggs, cream and sugar,
along with brandy and rum, either
or both of which can be replaced,
of course, with Canadian whisky.

FRANCE

◇◇◇◇◇◇◇◇◇◇◇◇◇◇◇◇◇

*France's global position as a wine producer goes without saying. But in whisky,
the country is just starting to gain a reputation.*

1984: Brittany reboots whisky production

During a reception at the French president's Élysée Palace,
a whisky called Le Biniou (from Brittany) proved to
be a huge success. 'Where can we get this?' asked the
distinguished guests. Problem was, production had stopped
several years ago. In 1983, Gilles Leizour took over the
distillery from his father and ordered new stills, spent two
months with distillers in Scotland, and then went back home
to Warenghem where he started up the first Breton whisky
in 1984.

A tradition of distillation

Even though whisky production is fairly recent in France,
the country has been distilling for years. France, after all, is
famous for pastis, Cognac, Armagnac, eaux de vie, absinthe,
and Chartreuse – all of which have been around for decades
in various regions.

A grain powerhouse

France also has one of the largest agricultural industries
in Europe. It grows wheat, barley, rye and corn – all basic
ingredients needed to produce whisky.

There's buckwheat in my whisky!

The Menhirs distillery in Brittany is not content simply
to borrow ideas from the other side of the English
Channel. Instead, it has become the only distillery in the
world to make whisky based on buckwheat. The whisky
is called Eddu ('buckwheat' in the Breton language)
– and is distinguished by its lighter, rounder taste.

France: a country of whisky fans

More whisky is drunk in France than any other spirit,
and it accounts for around 40 per cent of the country's
total annual spirits consumption: the equivalent of
2.15 litres (c.2 quarts) per inhabitant per year.

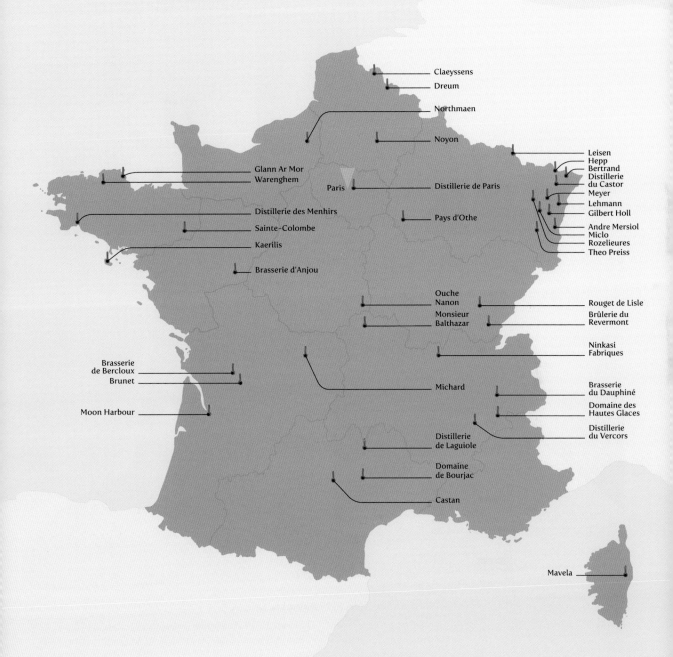

FRANCE

Claeyssens
Dreum
Northmaen
Noyon
Glann Ar Mor
Warenghem
Paris
Distillerie de Paris
Leisen
Hepp
Bertrand
Distillerie
du Castor
Meyer
Lehmann
Gilbert Holl
Andre Mersiol
Miclo
Rozelieures
Theo Preiss
Distillerie des Menhirs
Sainte-Colombe
Kaerilis
Pays d'Othe
Brasserie d'Anjou
Ouche
Nanon
Monsieur
Balthazar
Rouget de Lisle
Brûlerie du
Revermont
Ninkasi
Fabriques
Brasserie
de Bercloux
Brunet
Michard
Brasserie
du Dauphiné
Domaine des
Hautes Glaces
Distillerie
du Vercors
Moon Harbour
Distillerie
de Laguiole
Domaine
de Bourjac
Castan
Mavela

THE REST OF THE WORLD

Dozens of countries produce whisky, and often with great skill and creativity. Just because some are less known, that doesn't mean they lack distillery skills or instinctive know how.

ICELAND: A SPECIAL KIND OF SMOKE

There is no peat in Iceland. So enterprising distillers have adapted traditional methods used by crofters to dry meat: they burn sheep manure! Add to the equation a water supply of the highest purity, plus fertile lowlands for growing pesticide-free cereals, and you have all the ingredients needed to make great whisky.

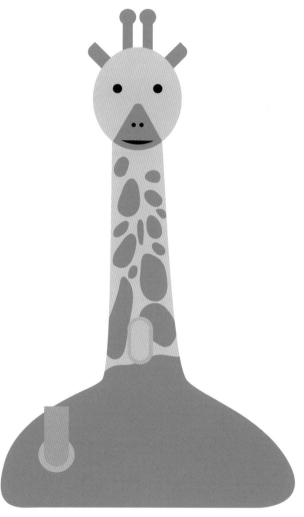

TASMANIA'S HELLYERS ROAD

Whiskey can be made at any latitude – even on the other side of the world. Tasmania has a distillery near Burnie called Hellyers Road, founded in 1999 by a group of dairy farmers who know their way around a still. In 2010, their single malt was dubbed best in the country by the Malt Whisky Association of Australia.

AFRICAN WHISKY?

There are just two distilleries on the African continent, both in South Africa: James Sedgwick in Wellington, near Cape Town, and Drayman's Brewery and Distillery in Pretoria.

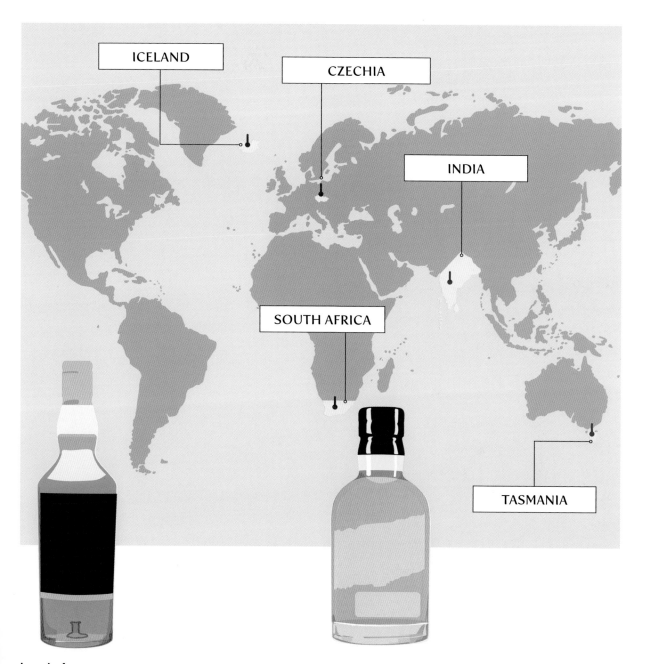

ICELAND

CZECHIA

INDIA

SOUTH AFRICA

TASMANIA

INDIA'S AMRUT LEADS THE WAY

Several distilleries make malt whisky in India, including Amrut in Bangalore, famed for its highly rated Amrut Fusion single malt, which is now sold all over the world. Amrut and other newcomers may start to change global attitudes about Indian whisky, which has previously been made mainly for domestic consumption using alcohol derived from molasses. Export sales of these non-whiskies have been restricted by the strict definition of which liquors can carry the whisky name.

COLD WAR WHISKY FROM CZECHIA

During the height of the Cold War, rivalry between East and West even extended to whisky. If capitalists could make single malt, then so could communists. A distillery was set up in the village of Prádlo (in the beer-brewing Plzeň region in what is now Czechia) and began making whisky. In 1989, when the Berlin Wall came down, the distillery was sold, and the contents of its ageing whisky casks were finally bottled in 2010. The result: Hammerhead 1989.

N°7
EXTRAS

There are still just one or two other things to leave you with, as you continue your journey of discovery: a handy glossary of whisky terms, a few striking statistics, a summary of some of the major players in the history of whisky (and whiskey) and, finally, a useful index to help you look stuff up.

WHISKY WORDS

If you love whisky, you may also come to love talking about it. Here are just a few of the more commonly used terms.

ABV or % vol.:
Alcohol by volume (ABV) is a measure of the strength of an alcoholic drink, and shows what volume of alcohol it contains. So 40 per cent ABV (or 40% vol) means the drink is made of 40 per cent alcohol and 60 per cent water.

Still:
Equipment, made of copper, that is used for distillation. The word comes from the Latin 'stillare' which means 'to drip'. The nature and quality of the distillate depend on the exact dimensions and profile of the still itself.

Low wines:
Obtained after the first distillation with a typical ABV of around 21 per cent. They are then distilled a second time to produce an alcohol with a 65–70 per cent ABV.

Cask Strength:
Indicates that a whisky was bottled at cask strength: i.e. at its cask ABV of 50–65 per cent, without the addition of any water.

Dram:
A unit of measure traditionally used for Scottish whiskies, and corresponds to a measure of 40–50ml (1¼–2fl oz).

Cask finishing:
Consists of transferring a maturing whisky from its original cask to another (often made of sherry-cask wood) and letting it age for several more months to obtain a wider range of aromas.

Tapping the bung:
Hitting the sides of the cask's stopper (the bung) with a mallet on all sides to open the cask.

Draff:
The residue of grain husks once all its sugar has been fermented out. It is used as animal feed.

Kiln:
A traditional oven used to dry barley as it germinates to produce malt. The kiln's roof is often designed in the shape of a pagoda.

Wort:
Sweet, lukewarm liquid made of soluble sugars coming from the barley dissolved in hot water.

Yeast:
Live organisms that allow fermentation to take place. Yeasts feed on the sweet wort and transform it into alcohol and carbon dioxide.

Mash tun:
Large wood or steel vat where the grain is crushed.

Grist:
Ground malted barley, used for distillation.

Perlage:
Technique of agitating a liquid to form bubbles. The more the bubbles hold their form, the higher the level of alcohol in the liquid.

Maturation:
A minimum of three years spent in the cask, where the wood adds taste and colour to the whisky.

The angels' share:
Alcohol lost to evaporation through the wall of the cask, typically two per cent per year.

WHISKY WORDS

Uisge beatha:
Gaelic term meaning 'water of life' (the equivalent of Latin *aqua vitae*.)

Slàinte mhaith ('SLAHN-ja VAH') or just **Slàinte**:
Gaelic for 'good health' – the equivalent of 'cheers', and something to say when you raise a glass of Scotch or Irish whiskey.

PPM:
Parts per million. Used to measure the quantities of phenols in whisky.

Peat:
Carbon-rich organic soil, used as a fuel; the smoke permeates barley with aromatics.

Single cask:
Single-malt whisky derived from a single cask.

Washback:
Tank in which the fermentation process takes place.

Spirit safe:
Traditional container of copper and glass, used by the master distiller to monitor and control the distillation process.

Quaich:
Two-handled whisky cup that has a strong link with Scotland's ancient heritage, used originally in ceremonial events.

WHISKY BY NUMBERS

We won't dazzle you with math, but here are nine useful figures to know.

In Japan, the Suntory brand accounts for 55 per cent of all whisky consumed.

Scotch whisky is the most widely consumed variety, shipping to 175 markets around the world.

The third Saturday of May is World Whisky Day. International Whisky Day is on 27 March each year.

It took the author of this book ten years to recover from a whisky hangover before being able to drink another glass of whisky.

Scotland is home to more than 20 million casks of maturing whisky – almost four for every person living there.

The USA produce approximately 37 million cases of whiskey each year, more than half of which is from Jack Daniel's and Jim Beam alone.

There are more than 5,000 types of single-malt whiskies.

A standard Bourbon barrel holds enough for 300 bottles of whiskey.

The largest tasting of spirits in the word (and recognized by Guinness World Records) gathered 2,252 participants. The event was organized by Whisky Unlimited in Ghent (Belgium) and took place on 31 January 2009. On the menu: Singleton 12YO, Cragganmore 12YO, Bushmills Original, Dalwhinnie 15YO, Talisker 10YO and Johnnie Walker Black Label 12YO.

WHISKY'S HALL OF FAME

Here's where to find the profiles of the men and women (and a cat) who have become part of whisky's history through the ages – and across the world.

MASATAKA TAKETSURU

(1894–1979)

◇◇◇◇◇◇◇◇

Methodical and scientific in his approach, Masataka Taketsuru is seen as the founding father of whisky in Japan.

Masataka Taketsuru came from a family of saké distillers. In 1916, when Taketsuru was 22, his employers sent him to Scotland to learn the secrets of whisky distilling. He visited many great distilleries of the time, including Lagavulin, and took detailed notes of everything that he saw, heard and tasted during his travels, even adding photographs and sketches to his notebooks to ensure nothing was missed. His earlier training as a chemist gave him a scientific approach, and he mapped out the whisky industry in Scotland in a way that had never been done before. Taketsuru's notebooks exist to this day.

Taketsuru fell under the spell of Scotch whisky, and also that of a certain young Scotswoman called Jessica Roberta Cowen, known as Rita. The pair married, and returned to Japan in 1920, but Taketsuru's boss dropped his plans for a whisky distillery. Taketsuru changed jobs, joining Shinjiro Torii, the founder of Suntory, where he set up the first Japanese whisky distillery: Yamazaki. Its first whisky, a blend, was launched in 1929, but failed to achieve the expected success.

Far from being discouraged, Taketsuru sought out a new location for his own distillery, one that contained some of the characteristics he had seen in Scotland. His research took him to the island of Hokkaido, where he set about constructing the Yoichi distillery. Nikka (the brand name dates back to 1952) was born.

INDEX

Illustrator: Yannis Varoutsikos

Yannis Varoutsikos is an artistic director and illustrator. He is plenty of other things, too, but that's another story.

He has illustrated several books on food and drink, including Wine It's Not Rocket Science *(2017),* Pâtisserie *(2016),* Coffee It's Not Rocket Science *(2019) and* The Complete Guide to Baking *(2017), as well as a French book on rugby.*

lacourtoisiecreative.com
lacourtoisiecreative.myportfolio.com

Author: Mickaël Guidot

Originally from Burgundy, Mickaël grew up close to the famous wine regions of Beaune and Nuits-Saint-Georges, where he spent a good deal of time in the bars and wine cellars of the region.

He left his homeland to work in Paris for various PR agencies, which is where he got acquainted with numerous brands of Champagne and spirits, and began to develop a more experienced palate and a lively interest in tastings.

With the aim of sharing his knowledge and discoveries, he set up the website www.forgeorges.fr in 2012. It was named in homage to his grandfather, who had died a few months earlier, and who always used to enjoy apéritifs with the family. He created the blog as a form of sharing and exchange, and has since developed a limitless passion for whisky, borne out by his own vast collection of bottles.

www.forgeorges.fr

An Hachette UK Company
www.hachette.co.uk–

First published in Great Britain in 2020 by Hamlyn, an imprint of
Octopus Publishing Group Ltd
Carmelite House
50 Victoria Embankment
London EC4Y 0DZ
www.octopusbooks.co.uk
www.octopusbooksusa.com

Distributed in the US by
Hachette Book Group
1290 Avenue of the Americas
4th and 5th Floors
New York, NY 10104

Distributed in Canada by
Canadian Manda Group
664 Annette St.
Toronto, Ontario, Canada M6S 2C8

First published in France in 2016 by Hachette Livre

Le Café C'est Pas Sorcier © Hachette Livre (Marabout) 2016
English translation © Octopus Publishing Group 2020

Cocktail recipes on pages 138–144 are from *The Bartender's Bible* by
Simon Difford (2015)

ISBN 978-0-600-63639-7

A CIP catalogue record for this book is available from the
British Library.

Printed and bound in China

10 9 8 7 6 5 4 3 2 1

For the French edition:
Artistic Director: Yannis Varoutsikos
Design: Les PAOistes
Editor: Charlotte Monnier

For this edition:
Group Publishing Director: Denise Bates
Assistant Editor: Emily Brickell
Designer: Jack Storey
Senior Production Controller: Allison Gonsalves
English Translation: Paul Carslake